Contents

Preface

We rarely feature group exhibitions that focus on one particular theme. The Van Abbemuseum mainly concentrates on monographic exhibitions or reflective moments within the oeuvre of a particular artist. This is not only a tradition that has developed over the years, but it is and continues to be a conscious choice as well. With many of the thematic exhibitions that have been presented in recent years, we have had the feeling that ultimately the focus was more on the ego of the exhibition organizer rather than on the work of the participating artists, too often the art has been reduced to an illustration for the text written by 'The Curator'. Such exhibitions are usually not the proper way to experience the essence of a particular body of work with any kind of precision and concentration.

But every now and then, artistic developments accelerate and shift. Sometimes there is evidence of substantial shifts taking place, because a younger generation — raised in a different, social, cultural and economical environment that has undergone fast changes — raises its head and commands attention for its own agenda. From these different backgrounds, distinct areas of interest and new frames of reference, new artistic priorities and accents inevitably arise, and the search begins for new, adept forms of articulation and presentation. Such a moment of metamorphosis requires also for the museum a searching for appropriate forms. A slowly unfolding series of one-man shows, such as those we

ID

Eija-Liisa Ahtila
VanessaBeecroft
Willie Doherty
Douglas Gordon
Aernout Mik
Tony Oursler
Sam Samore
Georgina Starr
GillianWearing

An international survey on the notion of identity in contemporary art

1996

Stedelijk Van Abbemuseum, Eindhoven

This catalogue appears on the occasion of the exhibition
ID - An international survey on the notion of identity in contemporary art
at the Stedelijk Van Abbemuseum, Eindhoven,
December 8, 1996 - February 9, 1997

have presented in recent years, would not fill the need to focus in right now and become involved in what is going on. For many of the artists with whom we have been in contact recently it is however too early for substantial monographic presentations. But we are also wary of the shortcomings inherent in the all too nerve-wracking mass exhibitions, in which dozens of artists who have little or nothing to do with each other are introduced simultaneously and hastily (usually by way of a single work) in a blaring potpourri that leaves everyone in the dark.

For this reason, at the basis of *ID* are three underlying principles. We want to begin with the introduction of what for us is a new artistic generation by choosing a limited number of artists. We do this not out of hesitation, but to make it possible to present several works from each artist so that the visitor is not inundated by too much all at once and can obtain a nuanced picture of each individual approach. Second, we do not want to have an exhibition in which one's acquaintance with one artist is immediately nullified when one steps into the next room containing a completely different story. Our aim was to find certain cohesive threads or themes which, although it may play a different role for each of the participating artists, nevertheless serves as a guiding principle - not as dogma or label, but as a common context against which these individual differences and unique identities can be seen in even stronger outline. And third, in contrast to the fashionable demand for new work (the answer to which is just as unpredictable for the artist), we have selected a number of existing works in consultation with the artists to make sure that the chosen theme in their work might be made as obvious as possible.

In this exhibition we wanted first of all to respond to the claim that for each of the artists and works in this group, one way or another, the central theme is searching for, defining or questioning the notion of identity in contemporary society; one's idividual identity, or that of the ordinary, day-to-day environment to which one reacts as an individual. From the specific Northern Irish reality of Willie Doherty to the reconstruction of the random unknown 'others' of Georgina Starr, or Douglas Gordon's inventory of all those 'others' who play some kind of role in the consciousness of his own 'me'. This art is not tautological or reflective on the ambiguity of the 'object' in art, this generation is interested in the awareness of day-to-day life and relations and is again falling back on a conceptual way of treating simple images. This is not art of the grand gesture or the individual esthetic. It is fragmentary, spontaneous, unassuming and, most of all, existential. We are looking at slices of daily life.

Jan Debbaut
Director

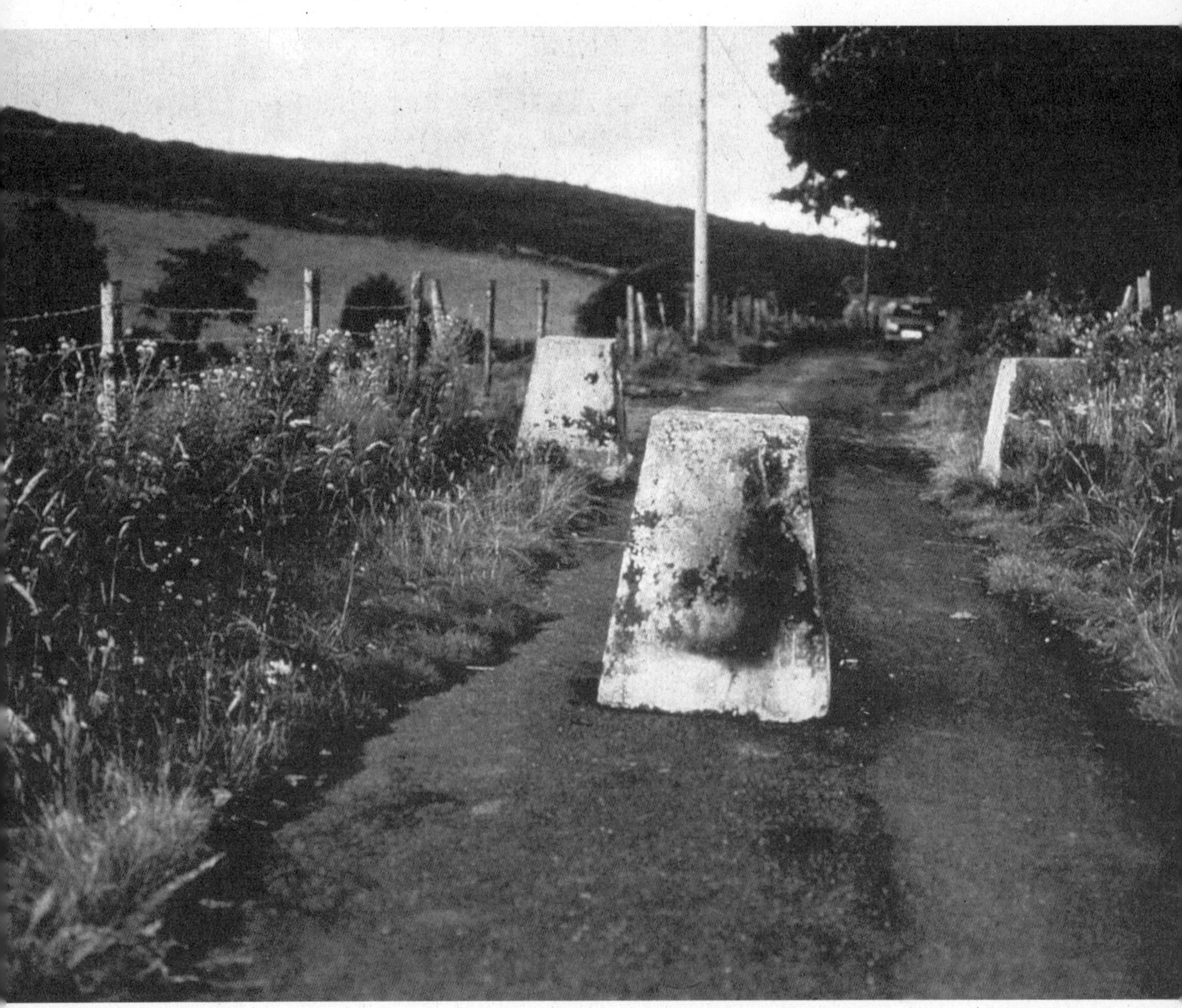

Willie Doherty
Border Road, 1994
cibachrome photograph mounted on aluminum
122 x 183 cm
courtesy Alexander and Bonin, New York & Matt's Gallery, London

"Dr Livingstone, I presume?"

Some remarks on the notion of identity in contemporary art

In 1871, after months of searching, the explorer and journalist Henry Morton Stanley found the missing Dr Livingstone in the heart of the jungle of present-day Zaire, and on coming face to face with his counterpart he spoke the famous words, "Dr Livingstone, I presume?" They are famous because there was no reason to be so cautious. Who else but Livingstone could Stanley have encountered in this hinterland never previously explored by whites? Famous too because that one sentence gives a splendid picture of the strong cultural identity of the British at that time. Present all over the world, from India to Australia and from Kenya to Burma, they remained true to such habits as tea-drinking on neatly trimmed lawns won from nature at considerable cost. Thus Stanley too remained — in the middle of the jungle and under extremely un-English conditions — a true representative of English politeness, of the culture of the stiff upper lip. Stanley's words were, however, wise ones. Not so much because the bearded, tired and emaciated person who stood before him confirmed that he was indeed Dr Livingstone, but because of the degree of uncertainty implicit in Stanley's question. Who or what, after all, lies behind a name, and does a proper name necessarily coincide with the person it is supposed to denote? Even if Dr Livingstone indeed turns out to be the man standing before him as a physical phenomenon, this does not mean that Stanley's idea of Dr Livingstone corresponds with Livingstone's idea of himself. And which judgment is more valuable: do you exist because you think you exist, or do you exist only through the eyes of others? Can you exist at all if there is no other human being to confirm the fact? Moreover, it is quite possible that the Dr Livingstone who departed from England bore little resemblance to the Dr Livingstone whom Stanley encountered in 1871. In fact it is very likely that during his many years in Africa Livingstone's ideas, feelings and attitudes changed completely, so that he would have undergone a radical change of identity. From this point of view, Stanley's reserve on meeting Livingstone, in the heyday of positivism, can be interpreted as a fundamental philosophical position.

To what extent does someone coincide with his physical manifestation? Suppose that while in Africa Livingstone had been brainwashed by a native tribe or, worse still, robbed of his brains and had another lot substituted for them. Would he then still be Dr Livingstone or not? And suppose that after this no doubt traumatic experience Livingstone sought refuge in other identities like a patient with a multiple personality disorder so that he could go on living without the constant awareness of a memory that he could not come to terms with. Who then is Dr Livingstone? At all events, someone with an identity different from the previous one. Is what matters the physical appearance, the facial features, the body, or is it the mind, not tied to any physical reality whatever? Or is there such a thing as a psychological substance? Of course, not all of these questions were going through Stanley's mind during that encounter in Zaire. They have been occupying men's minds for thousands of years. Who am I, where do I come from and how do I relate to other people? Isn't man, to stay within the bounds of Western thought, made in the image of God and thus the same as others? Or does each person have his own responsibility and is he thus different from his fellow human beings? Is there one self or various selves, and who decides? Can you change and still remain the same? Is identity a concept tied to a particular time and made up of countless different manifestations whose uniqueness lies in the sum of all of them?

In 1996 the question of identity is still topical and the answers still unsatisfactory. Despite the work of philosophers and scientists such as Charcot, Freud, Wittgenstein, Heidegger, Sartre and many others, the problem of identity remains as pressing long after Stanley found Livingstone. So it is hardly surprising that art, as the mirror of culture, has raised this question continually over the last one hundred and twenty-five years. Artists such as Dostoyevsky, Strindberg, Céline, Beckmann, Ibsen, Bausch, Konrad, Antonioni, Bacon, Wenders, among others, have been concerned with little else in their work. Yet there have been periods — quite recently — when artists preferred to leave the issue to other disciplines. So it is interesting to try to determine why in the present decade many artists again feel drawn to the notion of identity. Has something perhaps changed in art or in life? One admittedly gradual but fundamental change over the last ten years is the

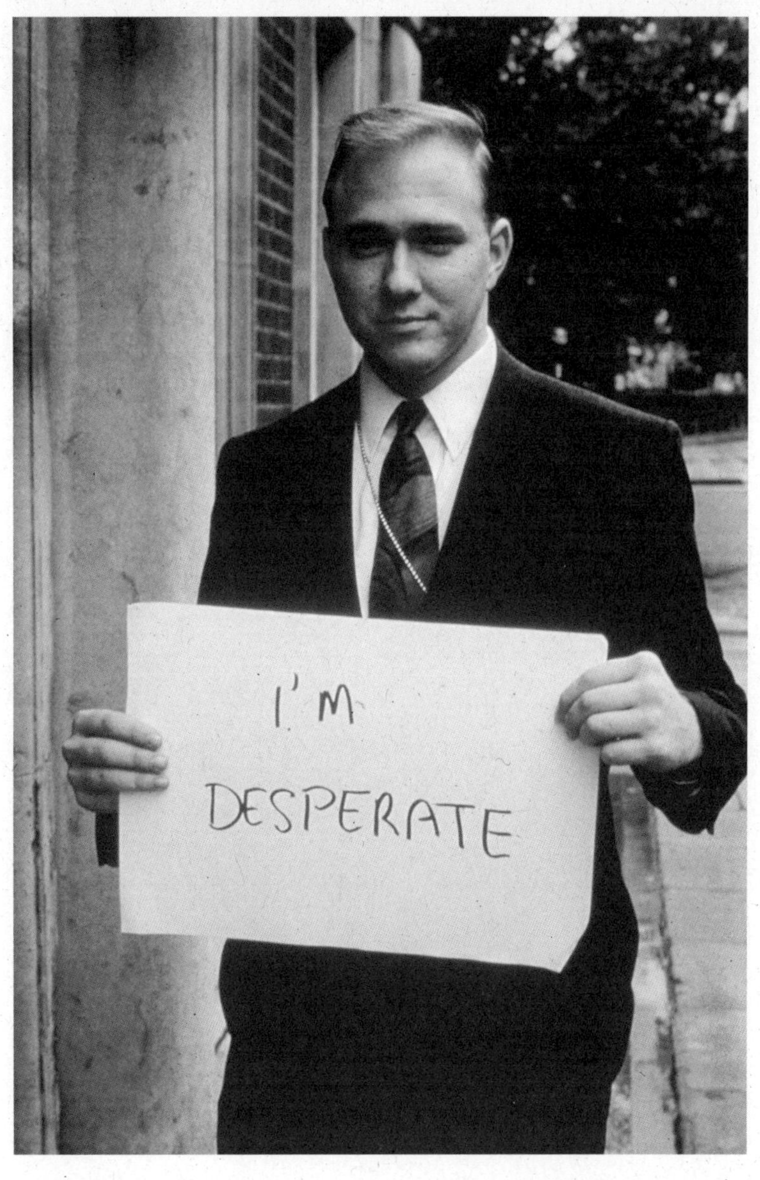

Gillian Wearing
Signs that say what you want them to say and not Signs that say what someone else wants you to say, 1992/93
C-print mounted on aluminum
30,50 x 40,65 cm
courtesy Maureen Paley/Interim Art, London

ubiquity of the media, and in particular the existence of a generation which takes this presence for granted. Never before has the range and reach of the media been so extensive and general. A constant stream of more or less similar information, advertising, (pop) culture, lifestyle and ideologies reaches practically every town, every village, every country and even every continent. These days Livingstone would have a hard time getting lost. Where could he find unknown territory to explore and who would not know his description from the media? Doesn't the loss of knowledge of the unknown mean that we loose sight of the unknown itself? Don't the media with their hitherto unknown speed of communication contribute to worlds becoming interwoven and to people resembling each other?

It is exactly here that there is an interesting development within the context of this account. On the one hand, as a result of the blurring of various structures which for centuries governed — usually unconsciously — the course of life, such as family, religion and political beliefs, people have had to rely increasingly on their own individuality. On the other hand, they are beginning to resemble each other more and more. The question is which tendency will prove the stronger: the urge to belong or the fear of losing individuality. It must also be borne in mind of course that the same media offer an enormous range of different lifestyles, kinds of music, clothes, religions and subcultures, etc. One has to ask, however, to what extent this is a true diversity. If the growth of these subcultures is caused in part by and enjoyed through those very media, doesn't it lose its intrinsic value? Doesn't sampling all these different 'dishes' become simply a matter of taste? Today this, tomorrow that, the day after tomorrow something else. Could it be that rapid changes of this kind have to do with a lack of direct experience? People know a great deal, see a great deal, but experience nothing, so that they can change (cultural) identity as easily as changing their clothes. It is the media — fed by the advertisers — which have most to gain from rapidly changing lifestyles, attitudes, cults and instant identities. Concepts such as lifestyle and identity have in fact become instruments of direct marketing.

In view of all this it should cause no surprise that artists are more than ever inclined to ask who they are and what meaning the whole concept of identity still has. Like no previous generation, they have grown up with the effects and potential of media techniques, so the use of film, video, photo and text is an obvious choice. Given that these techniques have a long tradition of dealing with social issues and personality problems, they seem more inviting and more appropriate than a brush and a can of paint for conveying the dilemma of individuality versus the need to belong as an important issue in the work of these artists. Moreover, the awareness of the huge manipulative power of the various media is a great challenge for many artists.

Together with the uniformity and instant identities created by the media, this

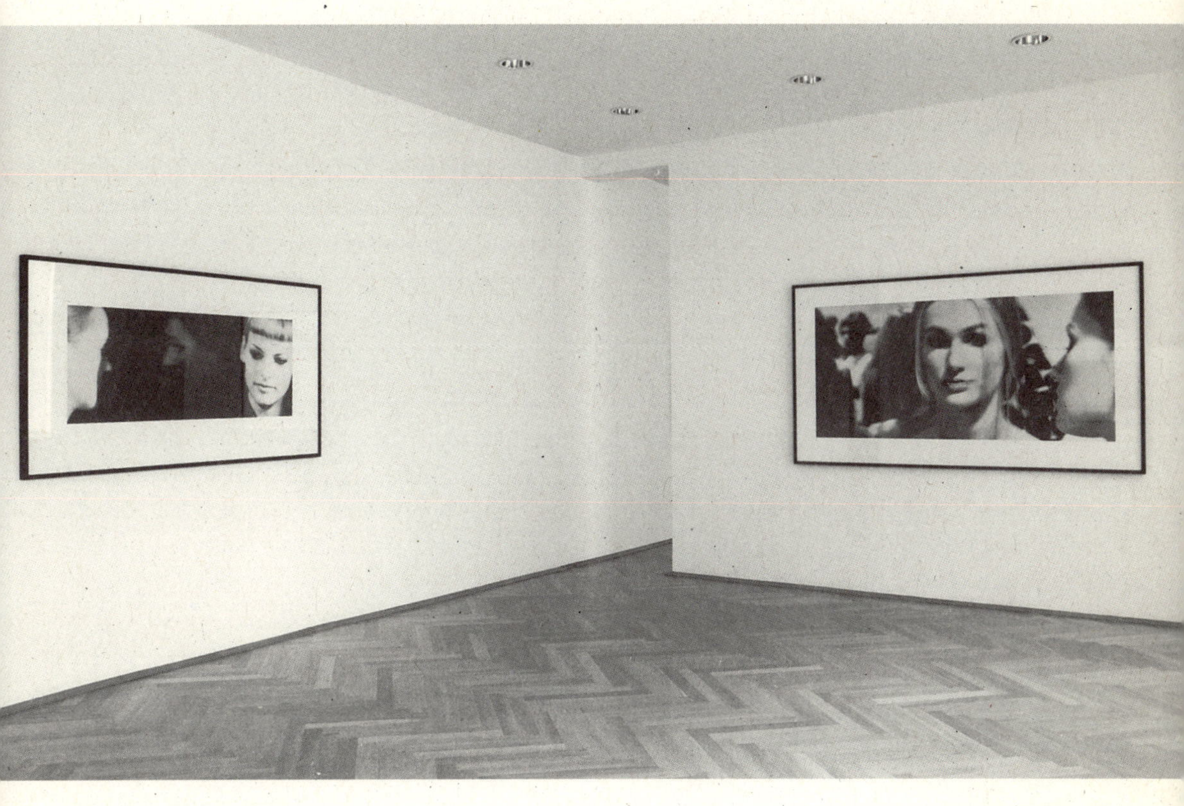

Sam Samore
Allegories of Beauty (Incomplete), 1995
Installation at Galerie Borgmann Capitain, Cologne (1995)

could be a reason for the renewed interest in the concept of identity in art. But who am I?

The artists

The ID exhibition presents a number of artists whose work is related directly or indirectly, as a main purpose or by- product, sometimes or always, to the concept of identity. One who is thoroughly aware of the situation described above is **Gillian Wearing**. For her work *Signs that say what you want them to say and not Signs that say what someone else wants you to say* (1992-1993) she asked chance passers-by on the street to write on a piece of paper what most preoccupied them. Then she photographed these people with their text. Showing the homeless and junkies, women out shopping, teenagers and businessmen, these photos and the answers present an honest and candid picture of their more intimate thoughts. Wearing's simple method ensures that as spectators we are made aware of the particular individuality of the otherwise anonymous passing crowd.

For *Take your top off*, three large photographic works of 1993, Wearing photographed herself lying in bed with a transsexual, both topless. In this way she questions not only the essence of the changed identity of transsexuals but also her own identity. Her work makes frequent use of the opposition between anonymity and individuality. By asking strangers to do or say something in the presence of her camera or video which they would normally keep to themselves, Wearing reveals the vulnerability of every individual and at the same time makes the viewer feel an empathy. Her work breaks down — if only for once — the anonymity and indifference in which people pass each other thousands of times a day.

Georgina Starr's work turns on her own personality. In her video installations, comics, scenarios and texts she herself always plays the lead role. In a light, playful and intelligent way Starr examines both her own identity and that of another. Thus *Getting to know you* (1993) and *Eric* (1993-1994) both literally hung on the quest for an unknown other. The way in which Starr conceives her works most resembles an exhaustive study in which she makes use of such diverse, surprising sources as dreams, stories told by others, found objects, fortune tellers, memories, songs, chance, misunderstandings and other kinds of 'non-information'. The result is that these works give us an idea of how we actually generate meaning. It is not the so-called 'main events' that give meaning to our lives but the ephemeral 'non-events' — they determine what we do, how we think and who we are. Starr's exploration of at first sight unimportant details shows how complex mechanisms govern someone's personality and how different individuals deal with the same stock of books, stories, meetings and sounds.

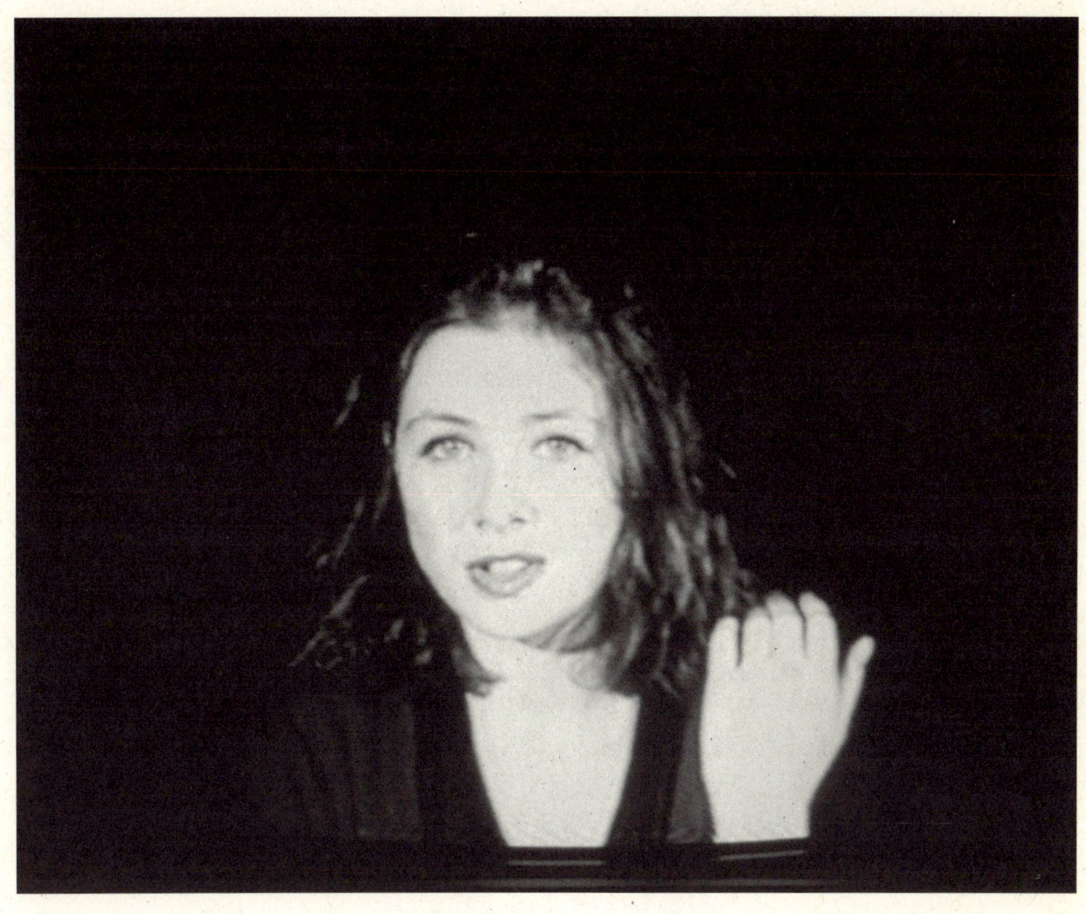

Getting to know You, 1993
installation, mixed media
courtesy the artist and Anthony Reynolds Gallery, London/Bloom Gallery, Amsterdam

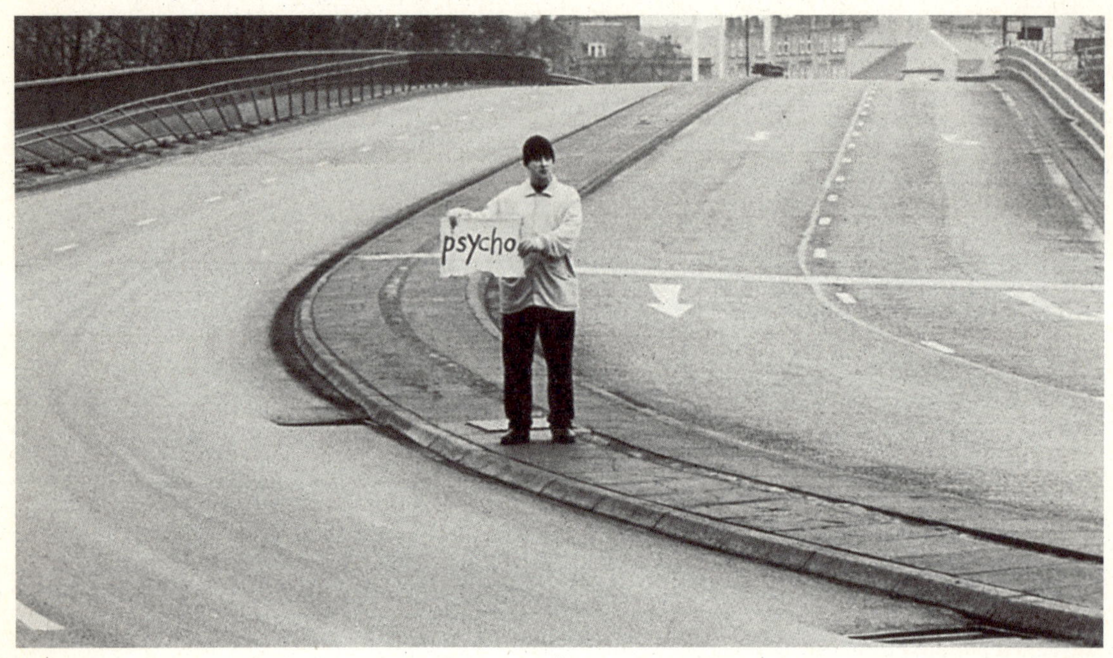

DOUGLAS GORDON
Psycho Hitchhiker, 1993
b/w photograph
46 x 59,5 cm
courtesy Lisson Gallery, London

List of Names (1990-ongoing), by **Douglas Gordon** is a list of all the people he can remember — at the time it is produced — ever having met. In 1990 there were 1400 names, now there are over 2500. The work shows how our system of cognition and memory works. Despite the apparently endlessly increasing number of new names, *List of Names* also reveals inaccuracy and the unconscious suppression of certain names in memory. Wall texts such as 'Those I do not know', 'Those I cannot know' and 'Those I would like to know' are directly related to this.

In his oeuvre Gordon frequently plays with the idea of attributing meaning. Many of his works are made in such a way that the meaning depends entirely on the beholder's own contribution, memory, powers of observation and sensitivity. No possibility of evading this is offered by the letters — individually addressed — which Gordon occasionally sends to various people. 'Nothing can be hidden for ever' and 'I remember more than you know' must have a confusing effect on the unsuspecting recipient.

Revealing what is subliminal and unconsciously thought and felt plays a role in works like *24 Hour Psycho* (1993) and *Predictable situation in unfamiliar surroundings* (1993) in which Gordon shows several scenes from the television series *Star Trek* and the whole of Hitchcock's film in extreme slow motion. Unhindered by the story, these works make us aware of the way in which these films generate their meaning, but above all of how we interpret and the role played by each person's individual memory. Without memory it would be impossible for us to attribute meaning: it ensures that we do not experience constant new impressions as a complete chaos.

Sam Samore's photographic works present extreme enlargements of human faces, usually in constellations of two or three people. The photos have a sharply lopped, horizontal format and show only faces in profile or full frontal and the space between. One striking aspect is that the eyes of the subjects never meet, never make contact, but always go past each other. In this way Samore is able to give his works a special tension. This derives on the one hand from a sense of the existential loneliness of all those individuals in an anonymous mass and on the other from the unusual cropping, which produces the suggestion of a short excerpt from a film or story. Who are these people, what is the relation between them, is there a relation, what are they doing? The photo calls on us to attribute a character, a story, an identity to those portrayed.

Samore's text works consist of series of unconnected words. They are often descriptive terms from which an image — different for each reader — of a person can be distilled. Samore distinguishes between so-called *Descriptions*, in which he himself constructs a person on the basis of endless lists of objective classifications such as sexual preference, weight, chest-waist-hip measurements, age, height and adjective describing personality and body features; *Portraits* consisting of a series of words obtained by selecting characterisations of a person from different sources of information; and *Names,* in which he gathers names and their corresponding phone numbers as they are listed in the phone book. These are names connected by genealogy, names selected by ethnicity, names determined by profession or names triggered by memory. More recent works have a freer structure and a poetic quality, which is strengthened by the fact that Samore puts his word works on transparent surfaces. Though to some extent comparable to Gordon's text works, Samore's series of words appeal not only to everyone's personal memories, but to everyone's ability to construct stories, people and characters for themselves.

In the performances of **Vanessa Beecroft** nothing actually happens. We see two, three, five or ten more or less similar girls, in more or less similar clothes, with more or less the same facial expression and make-up. Sometimes the girls are all wearing the same wig. Standing, sitting or leaning against a wall, they are above all present. The unusual thing is that in her performances Beecroft achieves a concentration which brings about both an intensification of ordinary, everyday poses and acts such as sitting and standing and a sense of alienation. In her first performance in 1993 she was herself the model for the type of girl of whom thirty filled the gallery. Beecroft brought in girls from the street who resembled her physically and in whom she recognised kindred spirits.

In Germany Beecroft used a character from Rosselini's film *Germania anno Zero.* This Edmund embodied Beecroft's own physical and moral weakness, just as all her characters have a direct symbolic and personal significance. Beecroft plays an intriguing game with identities, the motif of the double and finally her own identity. On the one hand her identification with different characters can be seen as a personal search for identity, something to go by, a model; on the other hand, the identification is immediately cancelled out by the multiplying of that one character. Are we all playing a single role or is the need to identify so great that we prefer to look exactly like each other?

Aernout Mik also makes use of living people in his works, but they cannot be described as performances. Not only because the presence of living people in his work has in principle no beginning or end, but chiefly because he uses them as chess pieces in a wide-ranging installation. The figures do not do much more than sit, lie, lean or sleep. Using living people makes it possible for Mik to create situations in which the visitor enters a space which is initially recognisable to him and conceivable, but on closer inspection turns out not to be so. In these installations Mik makes intelligent use of the reality of living persons who perform ordinary, everyday acts but who, because of the setting of the act and the often slightly distorted, 'heightened' reality, become alien after all. By leaving him

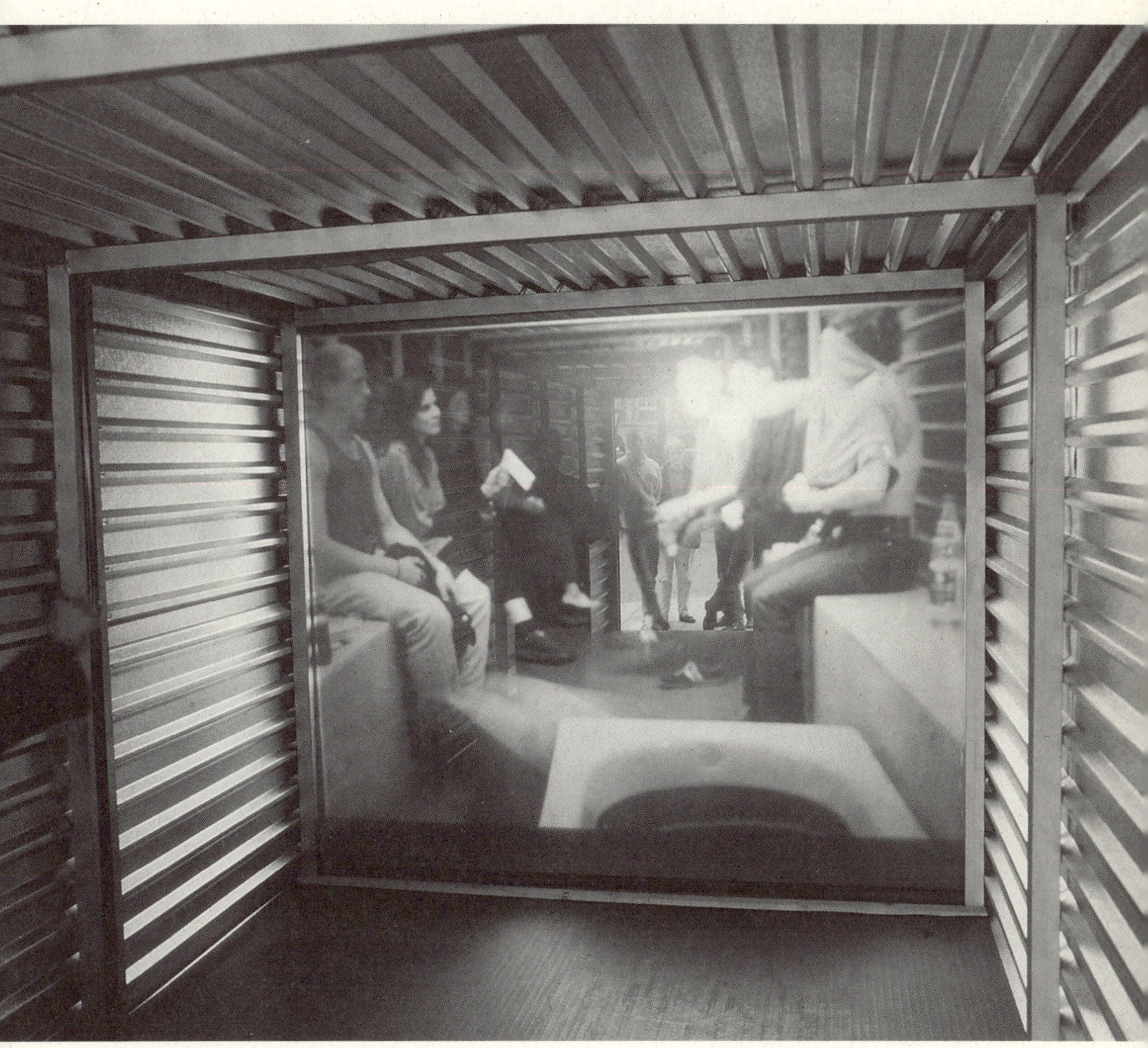

AERNOUT MIK
Langer oder Liegender Affe (detail), 1996
mixed media
200 x 250 x 2.000 cm

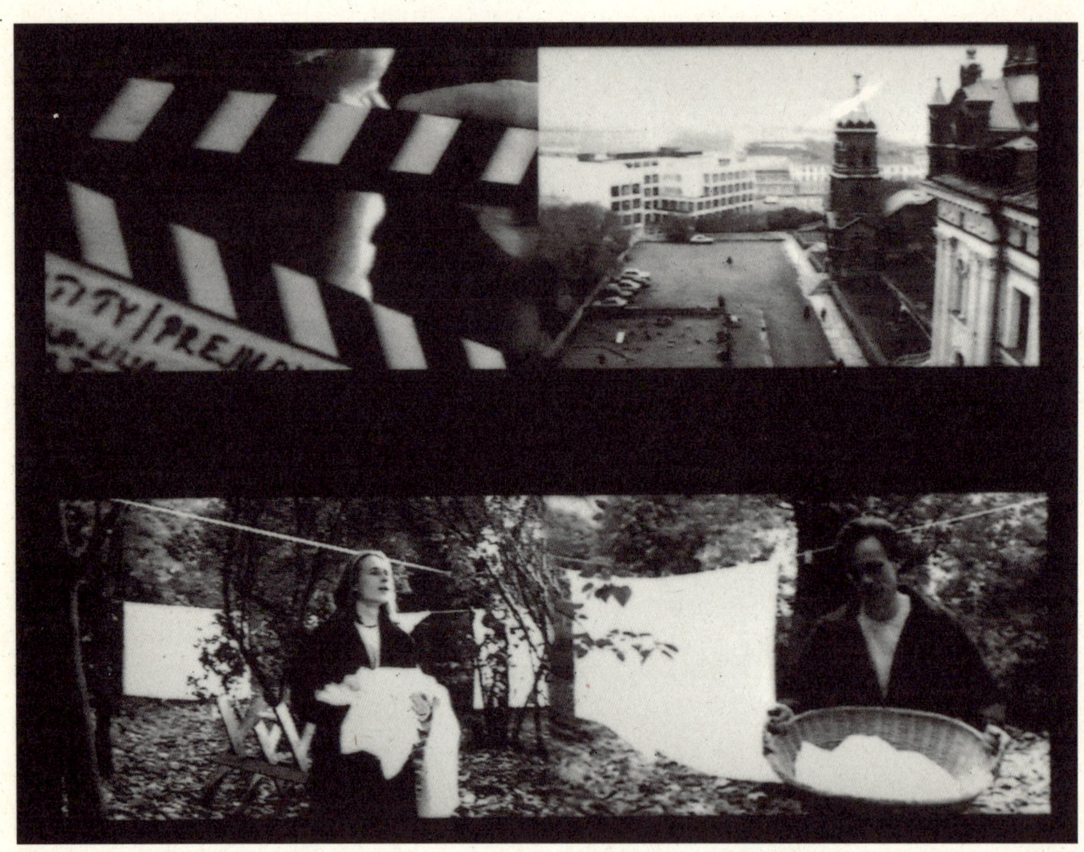

Eija-Liisa Athila
Me/We, Okay, Gray, 1993
S-16/35 mm film on video, b/w
video installation

no firm ground to stand on, Mik gives the viewer nothing to go by and forces him
to abandon his normal viewing and other behaviour patterns and think again.
Fluff (1996) consists of a filmed space with a number of people. The projection of
this film is installed by Mik in such a way that the filmed space and the real space
form one wall. Although the distance between the viewer and the filmed space is
of course considerably greater here, Mik succeeds in achieving a similar effect by
strengthening the non-real aspect of his filmed situation.

For **Willie Doherty** the role of the media in creating spurious, prototypical
identities is significant. Doherty refers to the conflict in Northern Ireland between
Catholics and Protestants, where reporting is such that instead of giving an
account it itself generates meaning. According to Doherty the media are guilty of
creating stereotypes, myths and clichés which the people themselves have
gradually come to believe.

In the video installation *The Only Good One is a Dead One* (1993) Doherty uses
some of the regular features of the media to visualise fear. On a projection screen
he shows us a night drive on an empty winding road in the countryside. On
another there is a shot from a still camera within a vehicle showing a city street at
night with passing traffic. At the same time you hear the monologue of a man
who keeps switching between being a target of violence, a possible next victim,
and being a stalker, an assassin surveilling and closing in on his prey.

Just as the media use the space between text and language and between image
and meaning for their own ends, so Doherty uses it to expose such techniques,
and above all their damaging effects.

The characters in the films of **Eija-Liisa Athila** are not easy to understand. They
speak with various voices, assume each other's personalities and have lines that
do not fit with their age. In *Me/We* (1993), a short film with the form and length of
a 90-second commercial, we see a young family hanging up the washing. The
story is told through the eyes of the father, who talks constantly and now and
again addresses the camera. The viewer is forced to identify with the father until
suddenly the role of narrator is taken over by the daughter. She speaks, however,
in her father's voice and as a projection of him. *Me/We* shows how the father
projects his identity on the members of his family, so making himself the master
of their identity. Something similar takes place in *Okay* (1993), another 90-second
film. In it we see a woman pacing back and forth in a room while she describes
her (sexual) relationship with her husband. Gradually her voice turns into that of a
man, and from what is said we can no longer determine which of the two is
speaking. In both *Okay* and *Me/We* Athila raises questions about the nature of
identity and the point at which one identity merges into another.

Tony Oursler's figures can in a sense be seen as an intensified form of the
moment described above in which someone takes possession of the identity of

another or in which someone loses his grip on his own identity. All his characters
seem to suffer from anxiety, depression and psychosis, with the individual having
to go to great trouble to hold his identity together and not lose himself. Oursler is
especially interested in the moment at which reason surrenders in the face of the
unknown and unprecedented depths of the soul. Does man show his true self at
such moments or has his true self been so damaged that it can only reveal itself in
a tormented state? In his work Oursler sketches an eye-opening and disturbing
picture of a society in which, because of the lack of coherent structures and ties,
the issue of identity has become the plaything of fundamental fears and instant
personalities created by the media. In Oursler's world no one can be sure of his
own identity or that of others. And man is reduced to an insignificant and
hopeless creature at the mercy of constant existential doubt.

Jaap Guldemond

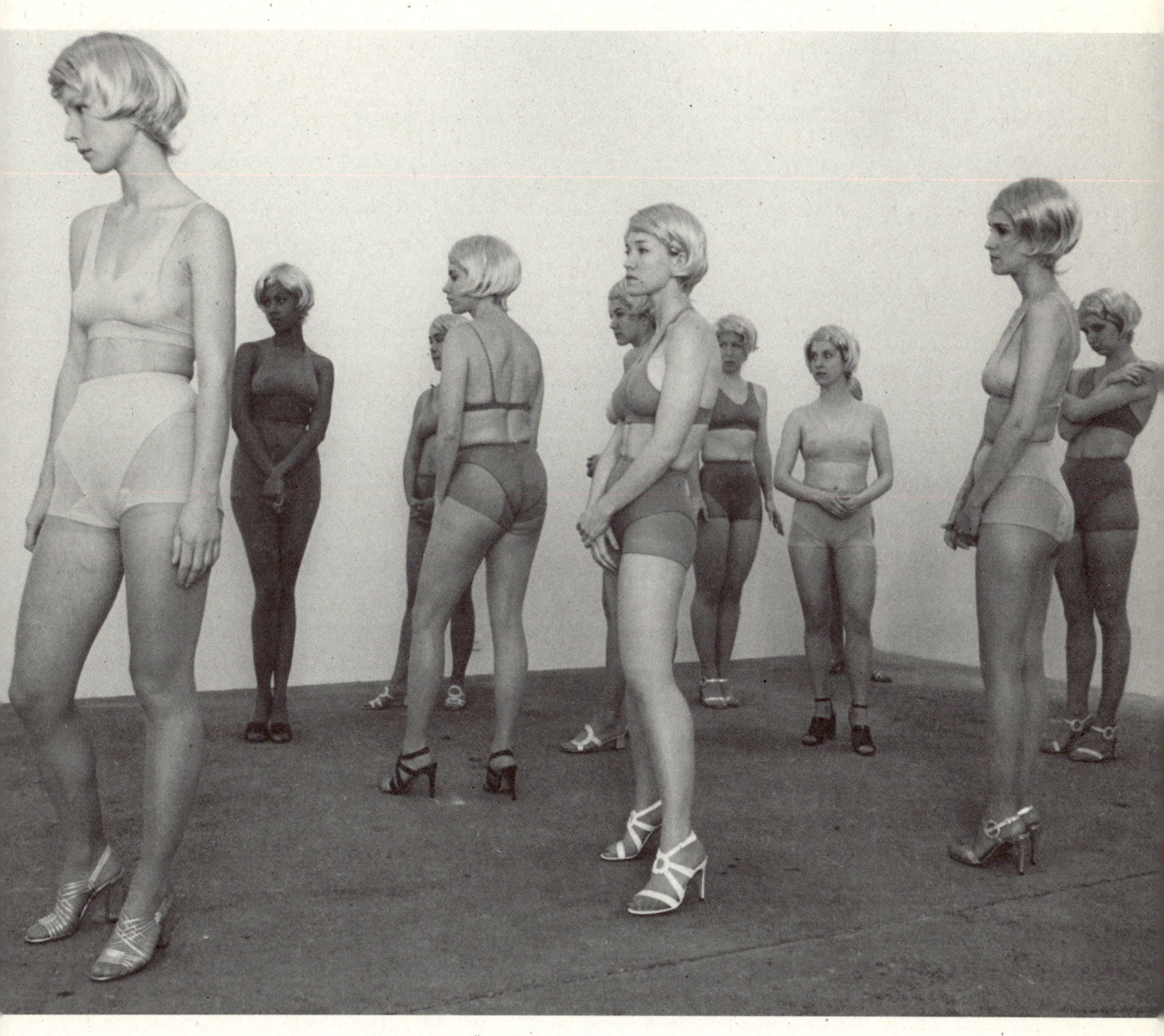

performance at Galleria Massimo De Carlo, Milan, 1996

A matter of identity

by Oliver Sacks

"What'll it be today?", he says, rubbing his hands. "Half a pound of Virginia, a nice piece of Nova?"

(Evidently he saw me as a customer — he would often pick up the phone on the ward, and say "Thompson's Delicatessen".)

"Oh Mr Thompson!", I exclaim, "and who do you think I am?"

"Good heavens, the light's bad — I took you for a customer. As if it isn't my old friend Tom Pitkins... Me and Tom", (he whispers in an aside to the nurse) "was always going to the races together."

"Mr Thompson, you are mistaken again."

"So I am", he rejoins, not put out for a moment. "Why would you be wearing a white coat if you were Tom? You're Hymie, the kosher butcher next door. No bloodstains on your coat though. Business bad today? You'll look like a slaughterhouse by the end of the week!"

Feeling a bit swept away myself in this whirlpool of identities, I finger the stethoscope dangling from my neck.

"A stethoscope!", he exploded. "And you pretending to be Hymie! You mechanics are all starting to fancy yourselves as doctors, what with your white coats and stethoscopes — as if you need a stethoscope to listen to a car! So, you're my old friend Manners from the Mobil station up the block, come in to get your boloney-and-rye..."

William Thompson rubbed his hands again, in his salesman-grocer's gesture, and looked for the counter. Not finding it, he looked at me strangely again.

"Where am I?", he said, with a sudden scared look. "I thought I was in my shop, doctor. My mind must have wandered... You'll be wanting my shirt off, to sound me as usual?"

"No, not the usual. I'm *not* your usual doctor."

"Indeed you're not. I could see that straightaway! You're not my usual chest-thumping doctor. And, by God, you've a beard! You look like Sigmund Freud — have I gone bonkers, round the bend?"

"No, Mr Thompson. Not round the bend. Just a little trouble with your memory — difficulties remembering and recognising people."

"My memory has been playing me some tricks", he admitted. "Sometimes I make mistakes — I take somebody for somebody else... What'll be now — Nova or Virginia?"

So it would happen, with variations, every time — with improvisations, always prompt, often funny, sometimes brilliant, and ultimately tragic. Mr Thompson would identify me — misidentify, pseudo-identify me — as a dozen different people in the course of five minutes. He would whirl, fluently, from one guess, one hypothesis, one belief, to the next, without any appearance of uncertainty at any point — he never knew who I was, or what and where *he* was, an ex-grocer, with severe Korsakov's, in a neurological institution.

He remembered nothing for more than a few seconds. He was continually disoriented. Abysses of amnesia continually opened beneath him, but he would bridge them, nimbly, by fluent confabulations and fictions of all kinds. For him they were not fictions, but how he suddenly saw, or interpreted, the world. Its radical flux and incoherence could not be tolerated, acknowledged, for an instant — there was, instead, this strange, delirious, quasi-coherence, as Mr Thompson, with his ceaseless, unconscious, quick-fire inventions continually improvised a world around him — an Arabian Nights world, a phantasmagoria, a dream, of ever-changing people, figures, situations — continual, kaleidoscopic mutations and transformations. For Mr Thompson, however, it was not a tissue of ever-changing, evanescent fancies and illusion, but a wholly normal, stable and factual world. So far as *he* was concerned, there was nothing the matter.

On one occasion, Mr Thompson went for a trip, identifying himself at the front desk as 'the Revd. William Thompson', ordering a taxi, and taking off for the day. The taxi-driver, whom we later spoke to, said he had never had so fascinating a passenger, for Mr Thompson told him one story after another, amazing personal stories full of fantastic adventures. "He seemed to have been everywhere, done everything, met everyone. I could hardly believe so much was possible in a single life", he said. "It is not exactly a single life", we answered. "It is all very curious — a matter of identity".[1]

Jimmie G., another Korsakov's patient, whom I have already described at length, had long since *cooled down* from his acute Korsakov's syndrome, and seemed to have settled into a state of permanent lostness (or, perhaps, a permanent now-seeming dream or reminiscence of the past). But Mr Thompson, only just out of hospital — his Korsakov's had exploded just three weeks before, when he developed a high fever, raved, and ceased to recognise all his family — was still on the boil, was still in an almost frenzied confabulatory delirium (of the sort sometimes called 'Korsakov's psychosis', though it is not really a psychosis at all), continually creating a world and self, to replace what was continually being forgotten and lost. Such a frenzy may call forth quite brilliant powers of invention and fancy — a veritable confabulatory genius — for such a patient *must literally make himself (and his world) up every moment.* We have, each of us, a life-story, an inner narrative — whose continuity, whose sense, *is* our lives. It might be said that each of us constructs and lives a 'narrative', and that this narrative *is* us, our identities.

If we wish to know about a man, we ask "what is his story — his real, inmost story?" — for each of us *is* a biography, a story. Each of us *is* a singular narrative, which is constructed, continually unconsciously, by, through, in us — through our perceptions, our feelings, our thoughts, our actions; and, not least, our discourse, our spoken narrations. Biologically, physiologically, we are not so different from each other; historically, as narratives — we are each of us unique.

To be ourselves we must *have* ourselves — possess, if need be re-possess, our life-stories. We must 'recollect' ourselves, recollect the inner drama, the narrative, of ourselves. A man *needs* such a narrative, a continuous inner narrative, to maintain his identity, his self.

This narrative need, perhaps, is the clue to Mr Thompson's desperate tale-telling, his verbosity. Deprived of continuity, of a quiet, continuous, inner narrative, he is driven to a sort of narrational frenzy — hence his ceaseless tales, his confabulations, his mythomania. Unable to maintain a genuine narrative or continuity. Unable to maintain a genuine inner world, he is driven to the proliferation of pseudo-narratives, in a pseudo-continuity, pseudo-worlds peopled by pseudo-people, phantoms. What is it *like* for Mr Thompson? Superficially, he comes over as an ebullient comic. People say: "He's a riot". And there *is* much that is farcical in such a situation, which might form the basis of comic novel.[2] It *is* comic, but not just comic — it is terrible as well. For here is a man who, in some sense, is desperate, in a frenzy. The world keeps disappearing, losing meaning, vanishing — and he must seek meaning, *make* meaning, in a desperate way, continually inventing, throwing bridges of meaning over abysses of meaninglessness, the chaos that yawns continually beneath him.

But does Mr Thompson himself know this, feel this? After finding him 'a riot', 'a laugh', 'loads of fun', people are disquieted, even terrified, by something in him. "He never stops", they say. "He's like a man in a race, a man trying to catch something which always eludes him." And, indeed, he can never stop running, for the breach in memory, in existence, in meaning, is never healed, but has to be bridged, to be 'patched', every second. And the bridges, the patches, for all their brilliance, fail to work — because they *are* confabulations, fictions, which cannot do service for reality, while also failing to correspond with reality. Does Mr Thompson feel *this*? Or, again, what *is* his 'feeling of reality'? Is he in a torment all the while — the torment of a man lost in unreality, struggling to rescue himself, but sinking himself, by ceaseless inventions, illusions, themselves quite unreal? It is certain that he is not at ease — there is a tense, taut look on his face all the while, as of a man under ceaseless inner pressure; and occasionally, not too often, or masked if present, a look of open, naked, pathetic bewilderment. What saves Mr Thompson in a sense, and in another sense damns him, *is* the forced or defensive superficiality of his life: the way in which it is, in effect, reduced to a surface, brilliant, shimmering, iridescent, ever-changing, but for all that a surface, a mass of illusions, a delirium, without depth.

And with this, no feeling *that* he has lost feeling (for the feeling he has lost), no feeling *that* he has lost the depths, that unfathomable, mysterious, myriad-levelled depth which somehow defines identity or reality. This strikes everyone who has been in contact with him for any time — that under his fluency, even his frenzy, is a strange loss of feeling — that feeling, or judgment, which distinguishes between 'real' and 'unreal', 'true' and 'untrue' (one cannot speak of 'lies' here, only of 'non-truth'), important and trivial, relevant or irrelevant. What comes out, torrentially, in his ceaseless confabulation, has, finally, a peculiar quality of indifference ... as if it didn't really matter what he said, or what anyone else did or said; as if nothing really mattered any more.

A striking example of this was presented one afternoon, when William Thompson, jabbering away, of all sorts of people who were improvised on the spot, said: "And there goes my younger brother, Bob, past the window", in the same, excited, but even and indifferent tone, as the rest of his monologue. I was dumbfounded when, a minute later, a man peeked round the door, and said: "I'm Bob, I'm his younger brother — I think he saw me passing by the window." Nothing in William's tone or manner — nothing in his exuberant, but unvarying and indifferent, style of monologue — had prepared me for the possibility of... reality. William spoke of his brother, who *was* real, in precisely the same tone, or lack of tone, in which he spoke of the unreal — and now, suddenly, out of the phantoms, a real figure appeared! Further, he did not treat his younger brother as 'real' — did not display any real emotion, was not in the least oriented or delivered from his delirium — but, on the contrary, instantly treated his brother *as* unreal,

effacing him, losing him, in a further whirl of delirium — utterly different from
the rare but profoundly moving times when Jimmie G. met *his* brother, and while
with him was unlost. This was intensely disconcerting to poor Bob — who said:
"I'm Bob, not Rob, not Dob", to no avail whatever. In the midst of confabulations
— perhaps some strand of memory, of remembered kinship, or identity, was still
holding (or came back for an instant) — William spoke of his *elder* brother,
George, using his invariable present indicative tense.
"But George died nineteen years ago!", said Bob, aghast. "Aye, George is always
the joker!", William quipped, apparently ignoring, or indifferent to Bob's comment
and went on blathering of George in his excited, dead way, insensitive to truth, to
reality, to propriety, to everything — insensitive too to the manifest distress of the
living brother before him.
It was this which convinced me, above everything, that there was some ultimate
and total loss of inner reality, of feeling and meaning, of soul, in William — and
led me to ask the Sisters, as I had asked them of Jimmie G. "Do you think William
has a soul? Or has he been pitched, scooped-out, de-souled, by disease?
This time, however, they looked worried by my question, as if something of the
sort were already in their minds: they could not say: "Judge for yourself. See Willie
in Chapel", because his wise-cracking, his confabulations continued even there.
There is an utter pathos, a sad *sense* of lostness, with Jimmie G. which one does
not feel, or feel directly, with the effervescent Mr Thompson. Jimmie has *moods*,
and a sort of brooding (or, at least, yearning) sadness, a depth, a soul, which does
not seem to be present in Mr Thompson. Doubtless, as the Sisters said, he had a
soul, an immortal soul, in the theological sense; could be seen, and loved, as an
individual by the Almighty; but, they agreed, something very disquieting had
happened to him, to his spirit, his character, in the ordinary, human sense.
It is *because* Jimmie is 'lost' that he *can* be redeemed or found, at least for a while,
in the mode of a genuine emotional relation. Jimmie is in despair, a quiet despair
(to use or adapt Kierkegaard's term) and therefore he has the possibility of
salvation, of touching base, the ground of reality, the feeling and meaning he has
lost, but still recognises, still yearns for...
But for William — with his brilliant, brassy surface, the unending joke which he
substitutes for the world (which if it covers over a desperation, is a desperation he
does not feel); for William with his manifest indifference to relation and reality
caught in an unending verbosity, there may be nothing 'redeeming' at all — his
confabulations, his apparitions, his frantic search for meanings, being the
ultimate barrier *to* any meaning.
Paradoxically, then, William's great gift — for confabulation — which has been
called out to leap continually over the ever — opening abyss of amnesia —
William's great gift is also his damnation. If only he could be *quiet*, one feels, for

an instant; if only he could stop the ceaseless chatter and jabber; if only he could relinquish the deceiving surface of illusions — then (ah then!) reality might seep in; something genuine, something deep, something true, something felt, could enter his soul.

For it is not memory which is the final, 'existential' casualty here (although his memory *is* wholly devastated); it is not memory only which has been so altered in him, but some ultimate capacity for feeling which is gone; and this is the sense in which he is 'de-souled'.

Luria speaks of such indifference as 'equalisation' — and sometimes seems to see it as the ultimate pathology, the final destroyer of any world, any self. It exerted, I think, a horrified fascination on him, as well as constituting an ultimate therapeutic challenge. He was drawn back to this theme again and again — sometimes in relation to Korsakov's and memory, as in *The Neuropsychology of Memory*, more often in relation to frontal-lobe syndromes, especially in *Human Brain and Psychological Processes*, which contains several full-length case-histories of such patients, fully comparable in their terrible coherence and impact to 'the man with a shattered world'— comparable, and, in a way, more terrible still, because they depict patients who do not realise that anything has befallen them, patients who have lost their own reality, without knowing it, patients who may not suffer, but be the most God-forsaken of all. Zazetsky (in *The Man with the Shattered World*) is constantly described as a *fighter*, always (even passionately) conscious of his state, and always fighting 'with the tenacity of the damned' to recover the use of his damaged brain. But William (like Luria's frontal-lobe patients) is so damned he does not know he is damned, for it is not just a faculty, or some faculties, which are damaged, but the very citadel, the self, the soul itself. William is 'lost', in this sense, far more than Jimmie — for all his brio — one never feels, or rarely feels, that there is a *person* remaining, whereas in Jimmie there is plainly a real, moral being, even if disconnected most of the time. In Jimmie, at least, reconnection is *possible* — the therapeutic challenge can be summed up as 'Only connect'.

Our efforts to 're-connect' William all fail — even increase his confabulatory pressure. But when we abdicate our efforts, and let him be, he sometimes wanders out into the quiet and undemanding garden which surrounds the Home, and there, in his quietness, he recovers his own quiet. The presence of others, other people, excite and rattle him, force him into an endless, frenzied, social chatter, a veritable delirium of identity-making and -seeking, the presence of plants, a quiet garden, the non-human order, making no social or human demands upon him, allow this identity-delirium to relax, to subside; and by their quiet, non-human self-sufficiency and completeness allow him a rare quietness and self-sufficiency of his own, by offering (beneath, or beyond, all merely human identities and relations) a deep wordless communion with Nature itself, and with this the restored sense of being in the world, being real.

1. A very similar story is related by Luria in *The Neurospychology of Memory* (1976), in which the spell-bound cabdriver only realised that his exotic passenger was ill when he gave him, for a fare, a temperature chart he was holding. Only then did he realise that this Scheherazade, this spinner of 1001 tales, was one of 'those strange patients' at the Neurological Institute.

2. Indeed such a novel has been written, shortly after 'The Lost Mariner' was published, a young writer named David Gilman sent me the manuscript of his book *Croppy Boy*, the story of an amnesiac like Mr Thompson, who enjoys the wild and unbridled license of creating identities, new selves, as he whims, and as he must — an astonishing imagination of an amnesiac genius, told with positively Joycean richness and gusto. I do not know whether it has been published; I am very sure it should be. I could not help wondering whether Mr Gilman had actually met (and studied) a 'Thompson' — as I have often wondered whether Borges' 'Funes', so uncannily similar to Luria's Mnemonist, may have been based on a personal encounter with such a mnemonist.

Moments passing by

When directors and film makers produce film, they are in a position where they can break up the conceptual apparatus around what we call reality, to make the parameters of reality come dangerously close to, or interfere with, fiction. In practice the task of the director also includes his being in charge of the actors and the production team, to be a bridge that leads from causality to an envisioned, artistic result. Such an artistic process includes a lot of people and presupposes communication and co-operation between the people involved.

A similar communicative attitude is reflected in Eija-Liisa Ahtila's films, in which the plot often turns around a group of people and their mutual relationships. In such a circle, relationships may be connected to the most intimate sphere: to family ties, love affairs and friendship, but they also depict relationships in a broader, social sense — for instance our encounter with the surrounding world and how forms of such a meeting are to be found, however incomprehensible the world might seem.

A garden. A clothes-line. A kitchen. A cup of coffee spilled out, as if in a dream, over a chequered oilcloth. Moments of familiar, everyday scenarios pass by before of our eyes but the balance of recognition has been displaced and climinated by the intrinsic complication of the action. *Me/We, Okay* and *Gray* (1993) are three black-and-white audio-visual short films that have been presented in a number of contexts: as autonomous works at the art institutions, together with trailers at cinemas and in commercials between the television programmes. There are formal similarities between these films and the commercial, where an idea or a piece of information is presented in a brief and compressed form. Ahtila's three films speak a language that is close to that of media, but unlike the over-explicit messages of the commercials they are also tainted by a quietly realistic and nebulous poetics. In the psychological and complex role-plays that take place between the characters, a number of remarks are made, just as funny as painful:

"If I could, I would transform myself into a dog and I would bark and bite everything that moves. Woof, woof ..."[1]

For what can one possibly do when words no longer work? How does one act when the parties involved have resigned themselves to such a degree in their attempts to reach out that there is hardly any point in trying to break the silence of the dying communication? The theme of *Me/We, Okay* and *Gray* revolves around questions about individual and collective identity: how is one affected by changes in the interior and exterior structures? Where does the ego end and where do the others take over? The ambivalent atmosphere is underlined by scenes where people suddenly change places with each other, where the actors take up each other's position and see themselves mirrored in the other. By taking over the voices of the others, they get the ability to tell a new version of the story with perfect lip-sync.

Eija-Liisa Ahtila calls her films 'human dramas'. It is an exact and apt title as the works deal with questions of the difficulty and lightness of the fact of being a living human being and the way these works insinuate that we are always in a process of learning, where the experiences of situations, events and encounters can only arise in life itself. The film *If 6 Was 9* (1995) is the result of a joint work between Ahtila and other people. The story that is told is fictitious but the dialogue is based on her research and on conversations she has had with close friends and with women in her surrounding. Thereby a sensuous fiction alternates with what could be details from the most private sphere. In fact, the script turns out to be neither fiction, nor biography; instead it is an indefinite mixture of private memories, of other people's experience, of real and fictive events. No specific person can claim to be the author since the story has developed out of a social situation where a choir of voices have been given the possibility to speak:

"Here I sit with my legs apart — like a small girl who has not learned anything about sex. Who has no idea of the fact that a woman must hide her private parts and lust. In fact I am 38 years old."[2]

If 6 was 9 tells the story of young girls and sex, about an age when sexuality is not yet a bond but is exclusively an expression of curiosity. It is an active form of sexuality, filled with expectations and characterised by a hunger for life to begin. The work is presented in a dark room where three projected images simultaneously moves the action forward in a pulsating rhythm. The cuts are exact and almost syncopated. Ahtila's characteristic way of combining motion pictures with different narrative devices and the way she connects this to a patchwork of different technical solutions (camera angles, tracking, treatment of lighting, moderate sound) produce an even flow of events where words and images can move independently of one another, away from and toward each other, sometimes running together. Eija-Liisa Ahtila's treatment of the screen gives her the opportunity to experiment with narrative techniques and the temporal perspective, and she is able to change the narrative, speed and linear temporality of traditional feature films, in favour of multilayered narratives with many possible readings.

Mats Stjernstedt

1. *Okay* (1993, s-16/35 mm film on video, b/w, video installation).
2. *If 6 Was 9* (1995, 16/35 mm film on video, colour, video installation)

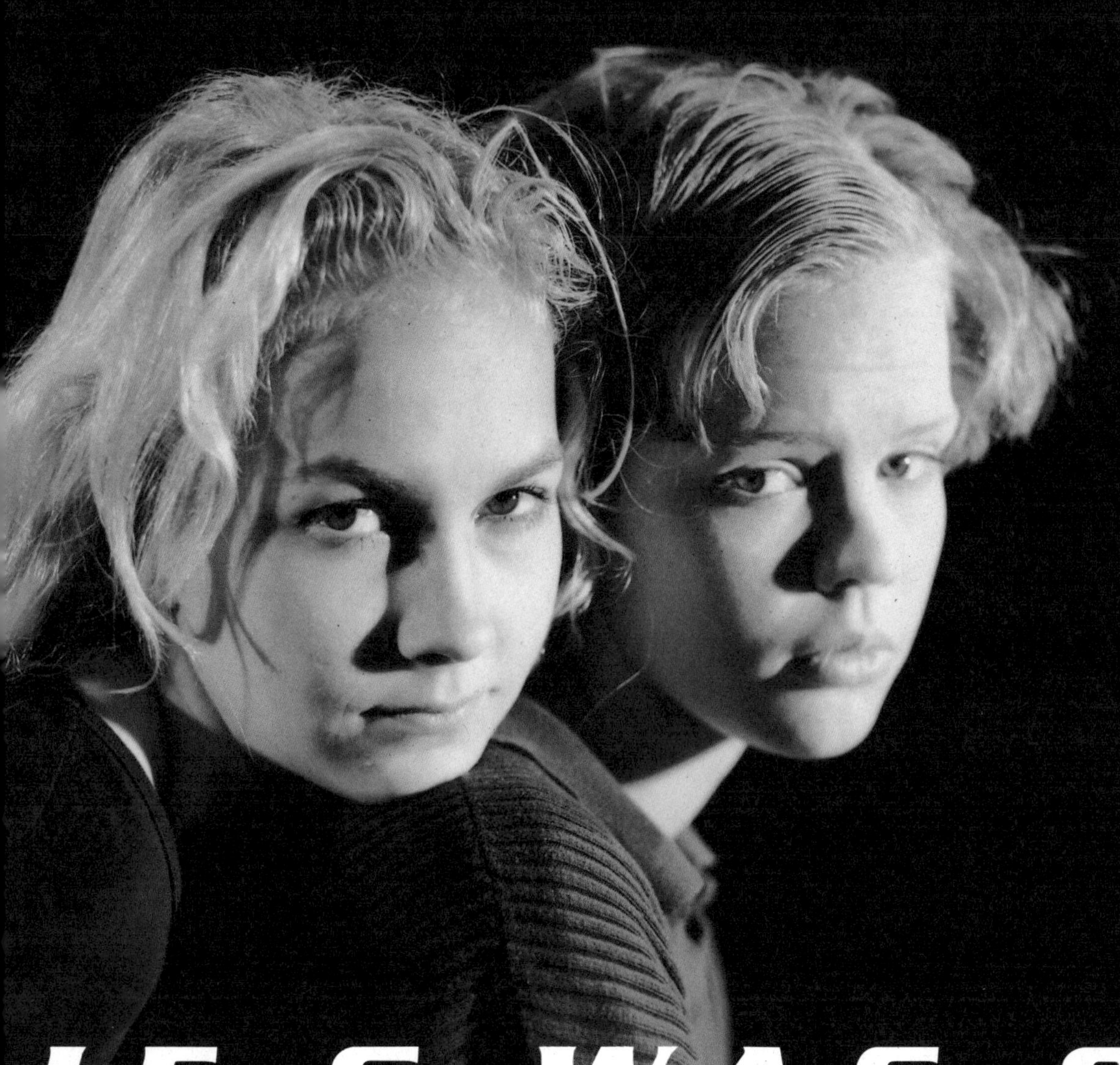

IF 6 WAS 9

A SPLIT SCREEN FILM ABOUT TEENAGE GIRLS AND SEX
BY *EIJA-LIISA AHTILA*

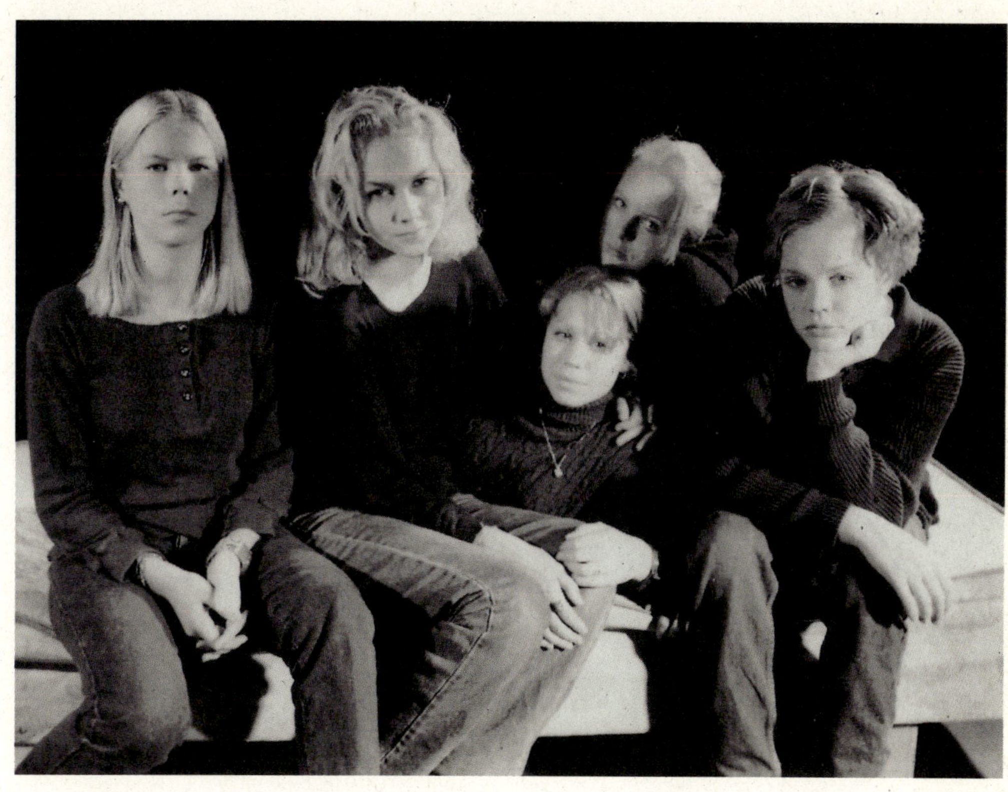

If 6 was 9, 1995
16/35 mm film on video, colour
video installation

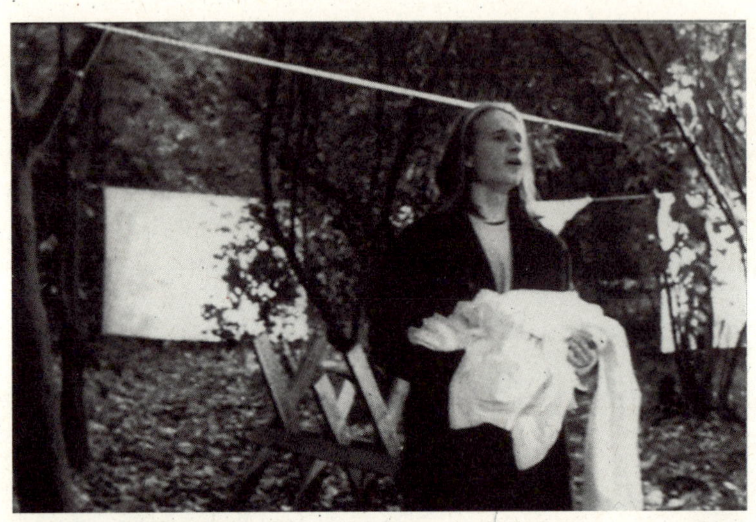

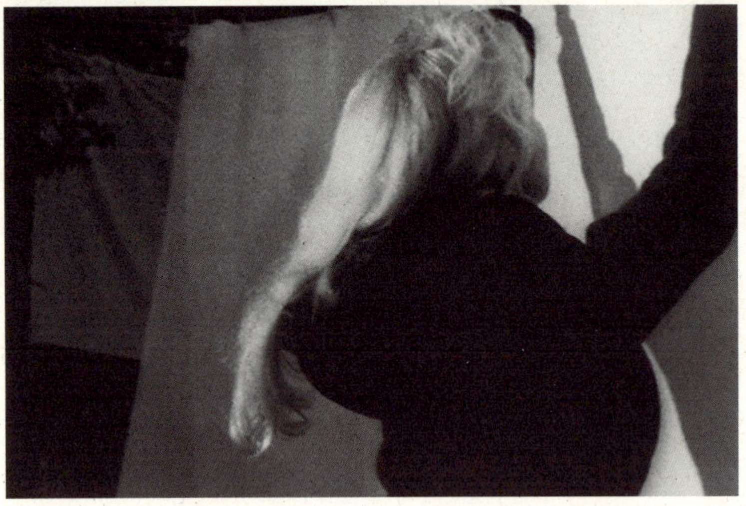

Me/We, Okay, Gray, 1993
S-16/35 mm film on video, b/w
video-installation

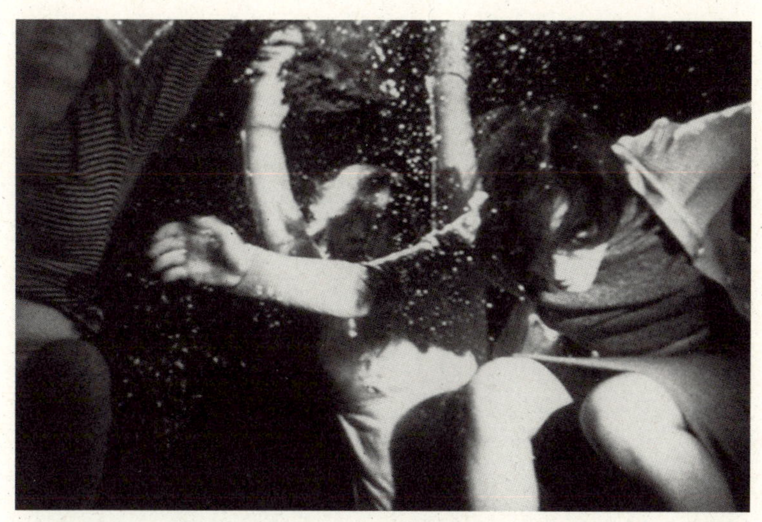

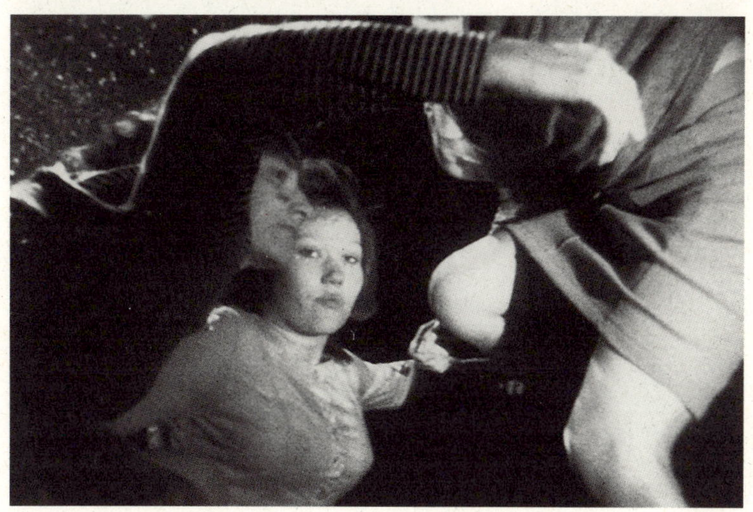

Vanessa Beecroft

Dream Girls

"I watch girls in the streets and try to imagine them as possible interpreters for roles they do not know of, which they reveal through the somatic tracts of their positioning in space while walking; sometimes I feel as if I had already seen them in a painting or a movie."

Vanessa Beecroft 1994

The common denominators of a Vanessa Beecroft performance are that a group of people, invariably young women, are placed in a room where they pace about, stand, sway, squat, or remain motionless, in accordance with the artist's wishes. For the duration of the performance, they are instructed not to talk. The girls wear dark blonde wigs — a bob cut with side parting — while their bodies are harnessed by all manner of tights, bras, girdles, and knickers. Some wear gold high-heeled shoes — in one performance, a girl sports a gold front tooth. The uniformity of colours in a Beecroft performance remains within a narrow band of hue — a twist of gold with silver, sometimes yellowish blonde wigs, offset by flesh-toned undergarments in beige, tan, and dusty brown. Eyebrows are plucked and heavily pencilled, while red lip-stick is invariably applied to resemble doll-like puckered lips. Their features appear Aryan, yet refuse to continue the notion of racial supremacy. It is equally likely that the girls appear Grecian, recalling fabled androgynous beauties bathed in Mediterranean twilight. Through the transformation of their physical appearance, the girls are objectified in as much as they resemble tailors dummies, fashion models, or simply *things* in a room. As visitors from Beecroft's imagination the girls appear alien, recalling the near-human androids, or 'replicants', envisaged by novelist Philip K. Dick and subsequently realised in the film *Blade Runner*. How can we fail to ogle them as they patrol the room in silence? After all, we have encountered these girls somewhere before...

1:5:96 A scene from Stanley Kubrick's *2001: A Space Odyssey*.

To the musical accompaniment of 'the Blue Danube' by Johann Strauss, a Pan American space shuttle leaves earth headed towards the moon. Dr Hayward Floyd, a diplomatic envoy for the National Council of Astronautics, slumbers in a comfortable passenger seat while his fountain pen drifts above the aisle, suspended in zero gravity. A cabin door opens and a stewardess enters wearing slip on shoes with velcro soles, a simple white jacket with matching slacks, and a bulbous white bonnet emblazoned with the Pan American logo (wardrobe by Hardy Amies). She walks up the aisle, gripping the floor with her shoes, plucks the pen from mid-air and returns it to Dr Floyd's breast pocket.

4:5:96 A scene from Andrei Tarkovsky's film *Solaris*.

Scientists discover a vast swirling cloud of 'thinking substance' in outer space, so-named the Solaris Ocean. Early research is thwarted when a reconnaissance vehicle enters the ocean and mysteriously disappears. In an attempt to retrieve the missing spacecraft, a young astronaut enters the cloud and returns having encountered what he believes to be alien life-forms — "I saw dwarf tress, hedges acacias, little paths...". Scientists decide to step up the Solaris Project and the ocean is bombarded with intense radiation from an orbiting space station. Shortly afterwards, scientists on board the station also claim to encounter alien life forms. Kris Kelvin, a young scientist, is despatched to file a report. Once aboard the station, he discovers his close friend and colleague, Gibrarian, has committed suicide, leaving behind a distraught video recording. The remaining two crewmen — Snow and Satorious — have become reclusive, rarely leaving their quarters. They seem unwilling to share their experiences and warn Kelvin to leave before he too is gripped by certain madness. Thereafter, Kelvin wanders the empty corridors in anticipation of alien contact. As he looks out into space through a portal, a woman wearing a blue chiffon negligée glides past. He glimpses her as she turns a corner. Where did she come from? Is she an hallucination? Kelvin is thrown into a state of confusion. Exhausted, he decides to rest. Aware of a presence in the room, he awakens to find himself in the company of his former wife who died 10 years earlier. Young, beautiful, untouched, wearing a brown suede dress and a knitted shawl, she crosses the room to kiss him. With her long chestnut hair tied back, she — the alien — is the materialisation of his memory.

30:10.95 A passage from John Wyndham's book *The Midwich Cuckoos*, 1957.

As [the children] approached I found the likeness between them even greater than I had expected. All four had the same brown complexions. The curious lucency of the skin that had been noticeable in them as babies had been greatly subdued by the sunburn, yet enough trace of it remained to attract one's notice. They shared the same dark-golden hair, straight, narrow noses, and rather small mouths. The way the eyes were set was perhaps more responsible than anything for a suggestion of 'foreigners', but it was an abstract foreignness, not calling to mind any particular race, or region. I could not see anything to distinguish one boy from the other; and indeed, I doubted whether, had it not been for the cut of the hair, I could have told the boys' faces from the girls', with certainty.
Soon I was able to see the eyes themselves. I had forgotten how striking they were in the babies, and remembered them as yellow. But they were more than that: they had a quality of glowing gold. Strange indeed, but, if one could disregard the strangeness, with a singular beauty. They looked like living, semi-precious stones.

Entranced by a Vanessa Beecroft performance, the thought crosses our mind that there is more to these girls than meets the eye.

Gregor Muir

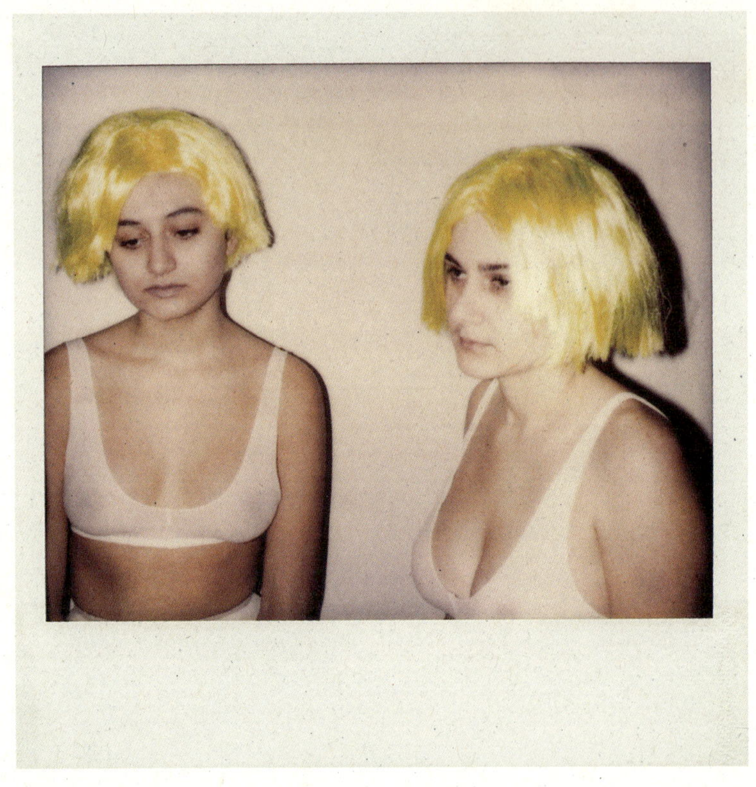

Untitled, 1995
Polaroid
performance at CAPC Musée d'Art Contemporain, Bordeaux

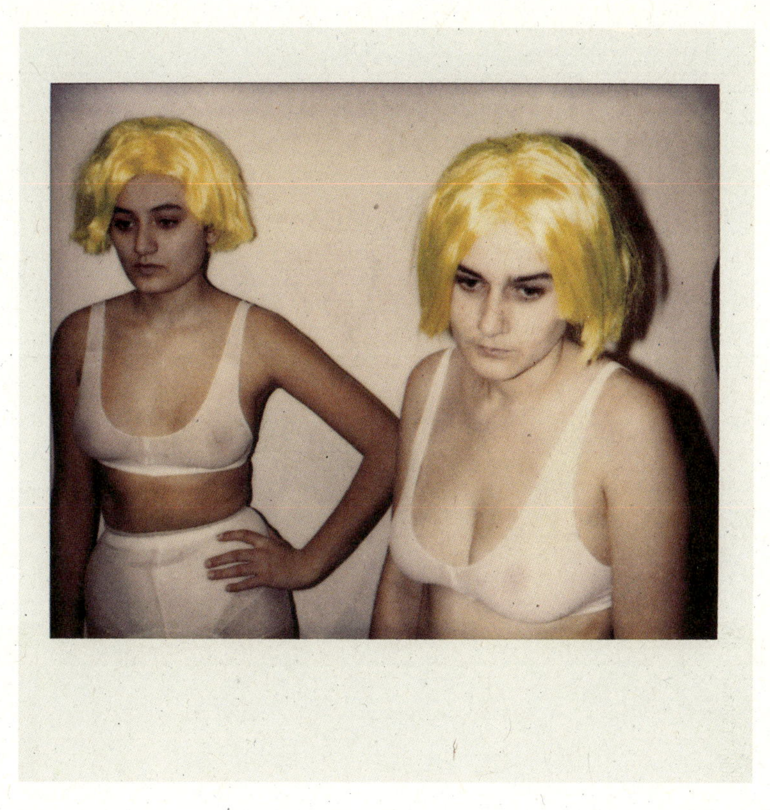

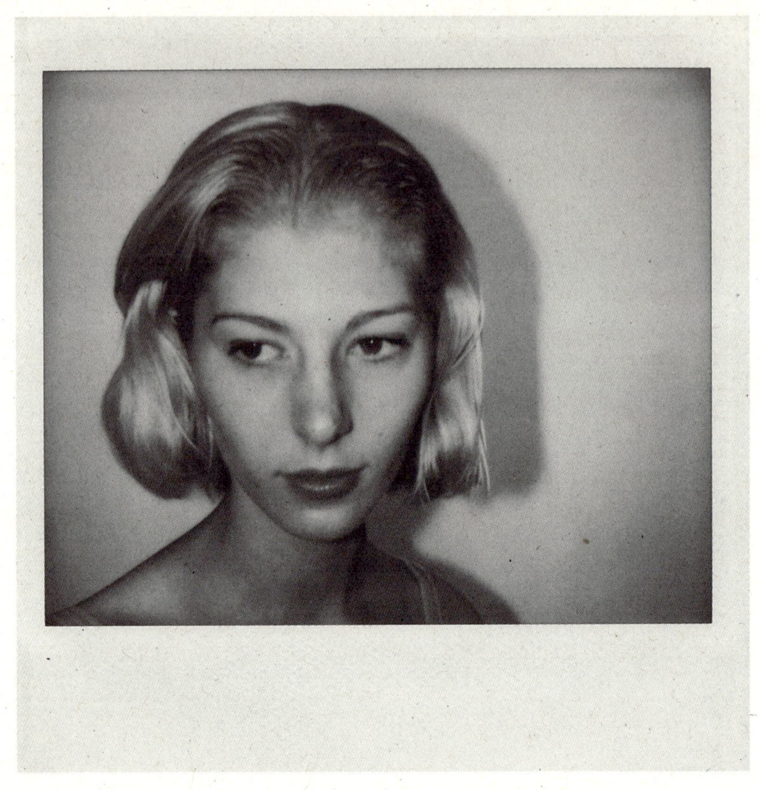

Untitled, 1995
Polaroid
performance at Galleria Massimo De Carlo, Milan

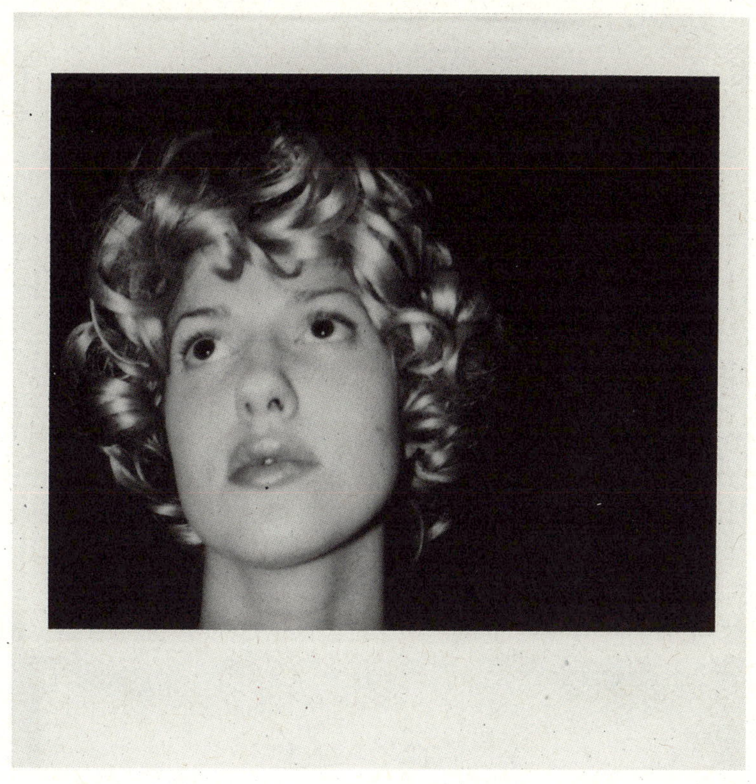

Untitled, 1995
Polaroid
performance at ICA, Philadelphia

The only good one is a dead one

Willie Doherty's work is deeply concerned with the way that images disseminated through the mass media manipulate our interpretations of events and other people, particularly in the construction of notions of ethnic or national identities. Thus, his work functions in a critical and dialectical relation with the codes of newspaper reportage, TV documentary and the kinds of promotional advertising to be found in tourist brochures, whose conventions are rooted in the picturesque and romantic sublime. For the most part, Doherty's themes and subjects are drawn from his own local experience: the sociopolitical and historical circumstances of the city of Derry and its environs[1]. Derry's position is ambivalent: this walled city was sequestered to the 'North' — a political designation reflected in the traditional positioning of Protestants inside the city walls and Catholics without — by virtue of its symbolic value to the Unionist cause[2], when topographically it 'belongs' to Donegal, a county in the 'South' but geographically the most northern part of Ireland. This ambivalence or redoubled identity is reflected in the structural relations of Doherty's work.

That the artist focuses his attention on his own background stems in part from the need to speak against the silence imposed until very recently on the Catholic community (identified as predominantly Republican) under Unionist and British rule, whose various strategies to deny it a political voice culminated in the notorious 1988 British government media broadcast ban and the rescinding of the 'right to silence' of prisoners charged with 'acts of terrorism'. Aimed primarily at silencing the political party Sinn Fein, these measures foreclosed any inclusive debate, effectively criminalizing dissent and thereby aggravating Republican grievances. *Self-representation* — and all that this implies in terms of self-respect and the sense of having some control over one's own destiny — has therefore been a primary goal in the political struggle of the Catholic community.

This does not mean, however, that Doherty's work seeks to present a more 'authentic' vision than any other representation of Ireland, on the contrary, it is precisely *the question of authenticity* that is at issue here. It is an officially unacknowledged fact that the reportage from 'foreign' journalists sent into Northern Ireland since the 'Troubles' re-ignited in the late sixties has been variously compromised by political bias, historical ignorance, neo-liberal sentimentalism, and a general failure (or a lack of will) to grasp the complexity of the situation. The 'Troubles', as Liz Curtis has pointed out[3,] have been as much a propaganda war as an armed conflict, exacerbated by official *dis*information and self-censorship on the part of broadcasting media fearing government reprisals if a more balanced analysis were made available for public debate. At the same time it is also true that proximity is no guarantee of truth either: rethoric from inside the Republican and Unionist sides of the conflict, has been equally fraught with ingrained myths, bigotry and entrenched positions.

In *Native Disorders I, II* and *III* (1991) we are presented with no more than a close up shot of different rock formations, the third completely covered in a dense mat of green seaweed. It is the caption that locates us; we are looking at images taken in the South, on the shorelines of the Aran Isles, but also of Co. Donegal, a stone's throw from Derry. What therefore is encrypted in the legends overlying the images and displaced onto the landscape — *Primitive Lines/ Loathing; Untamed Forms/ Despairing; Barbaric Mire/ Weeping* — is the doubled Irish imaginary as it is structured from the perspective of both the colonizer and the colonized. We become aware that landscape, far from being a neutral or transparent image of some primal nature, is deeply encoded, not only with marks of ownership and use, but also with myths of ethnic identity and nationhood. In the history of Anglo-Irish relations, the character of the landscape came to signify that of the Irish people themselves in terms of the colonial disposition of self/other, civilized/savage. Thus, those elements in nature that could not be appropriated or 'tamed' by the colonial power — the uncultivated bogs and stony uplands, the unpredictability of the weather, a Celtic social pre-history indelibly engraved in the topography and its vegetation — were projected onto the identity of the people as capricious, wild and illegible.

From the point of view of the Irish self-image, a long standing nostalgia for a lost, Celtic past, perpetuated through several narrative myth cycles attached to the land, has always inscribed the blood-and-sacrifice Irish struggle for a national identity. "They represent the blood and sweat of countless generations. For all this land is 'made' land, hand made", as the voice-over says in *They're All the Same,* 1991. The legacy of this metaphysics of Irish essence persists in the touristic promotion of a romanticized wild and 'unspoiled' landscape, through which the 'Troubles' themselves pass into the mythic narrative of heroic struggle[4], a manoeuvre that loses sight of historical process and, by extension, the capacity to reinvent cultural identities.

Jean Fisher

1.Within the history of England's development as a modern nation-state, Ireland was its first colony and the Six Counties which comprise Northern Ireland, withheld by the British Crown when Ireland gained independance in 1921, is anachronistically its last.

2.In 1688, faced with the prospect of being a Catholic garrison town, 13 of Derry's apprentice boys shut the city gates against the troops of King James II to await those of the newly appointed king, the Protestant William of Orange, an event that maintained the city in Protestant hands, and hence a part of Unionism's heroic mythology.

3.Liz Curtis, *Ireland and the Propaganda War: The Britisch Media and the 'Battle for Hearts and Minds',* London and Sydney, Pluto Press, 1984.

4.Bill Rolston, *'Selling tourism in a country at war',* Race and Class, 37, 1, 1995, pp. 23-40.

PAGE 50-51
Incident, 1993
cibachrome photograph mounted on aluminum
122 x 183 cm
courtesy Alexander and Bonin, New York & Matt's Gallery, London
PAGE 52-53
They're all the Same, 1991
installation with slide projection with audio text
Collection Goetz, Munich

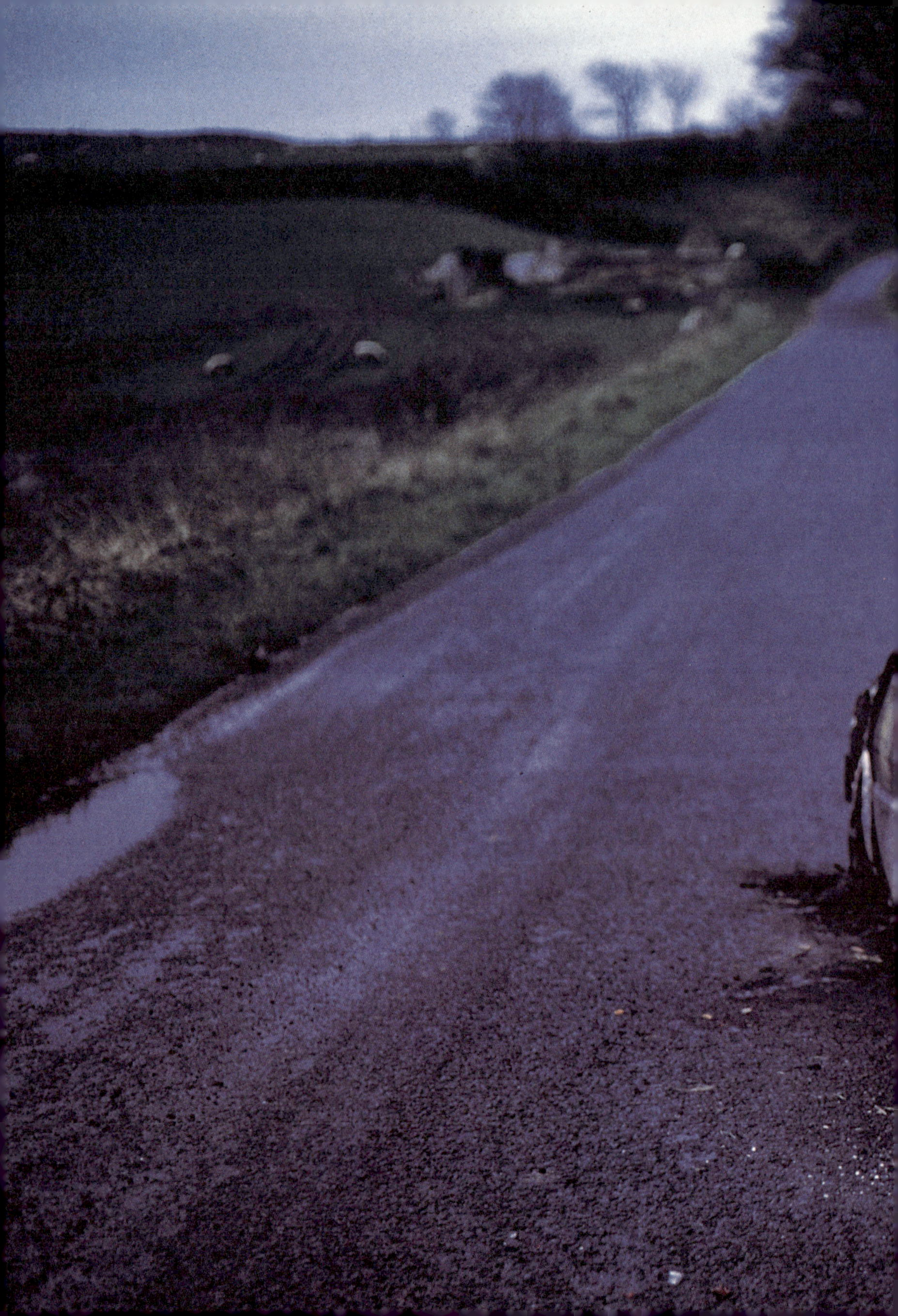

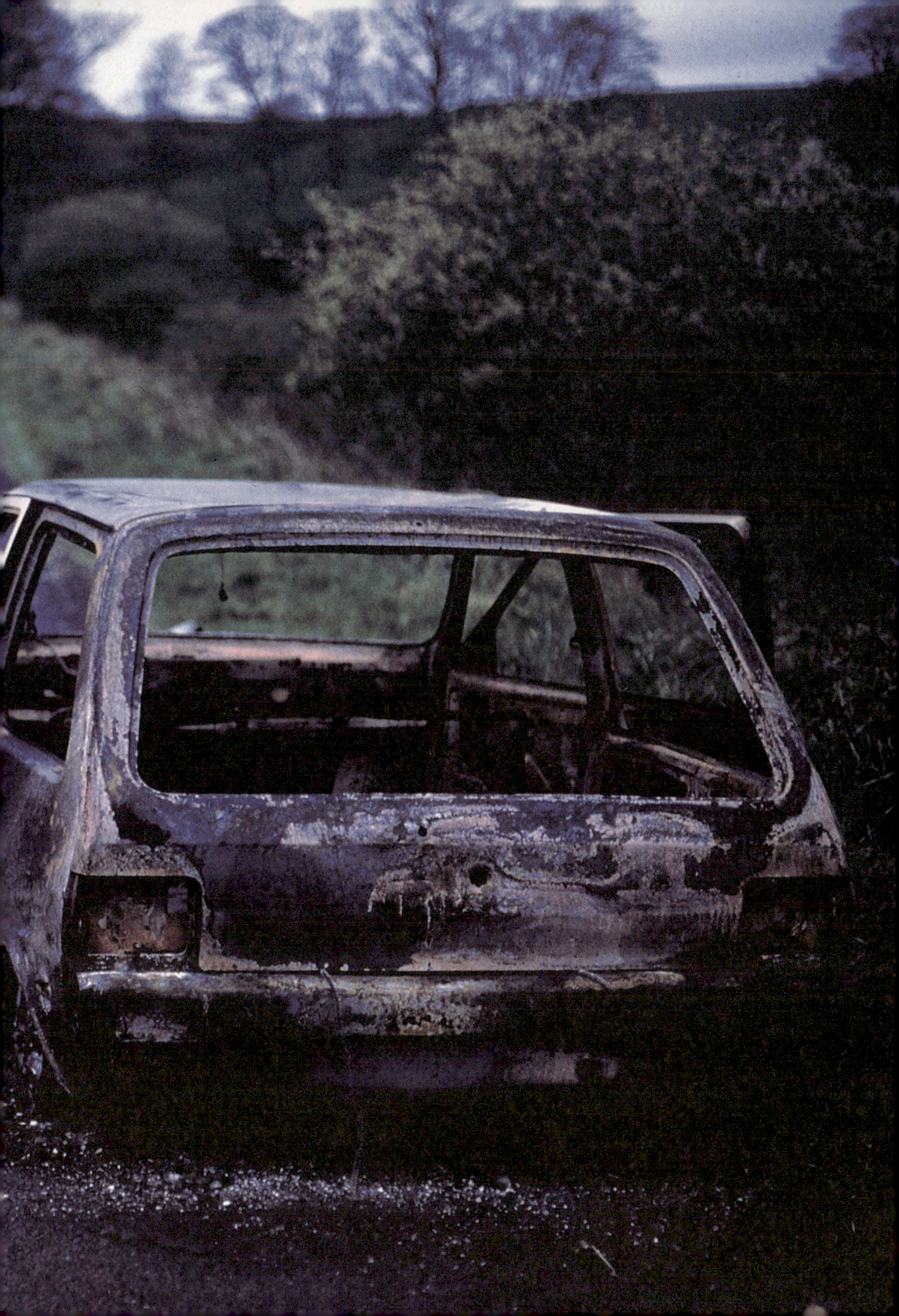

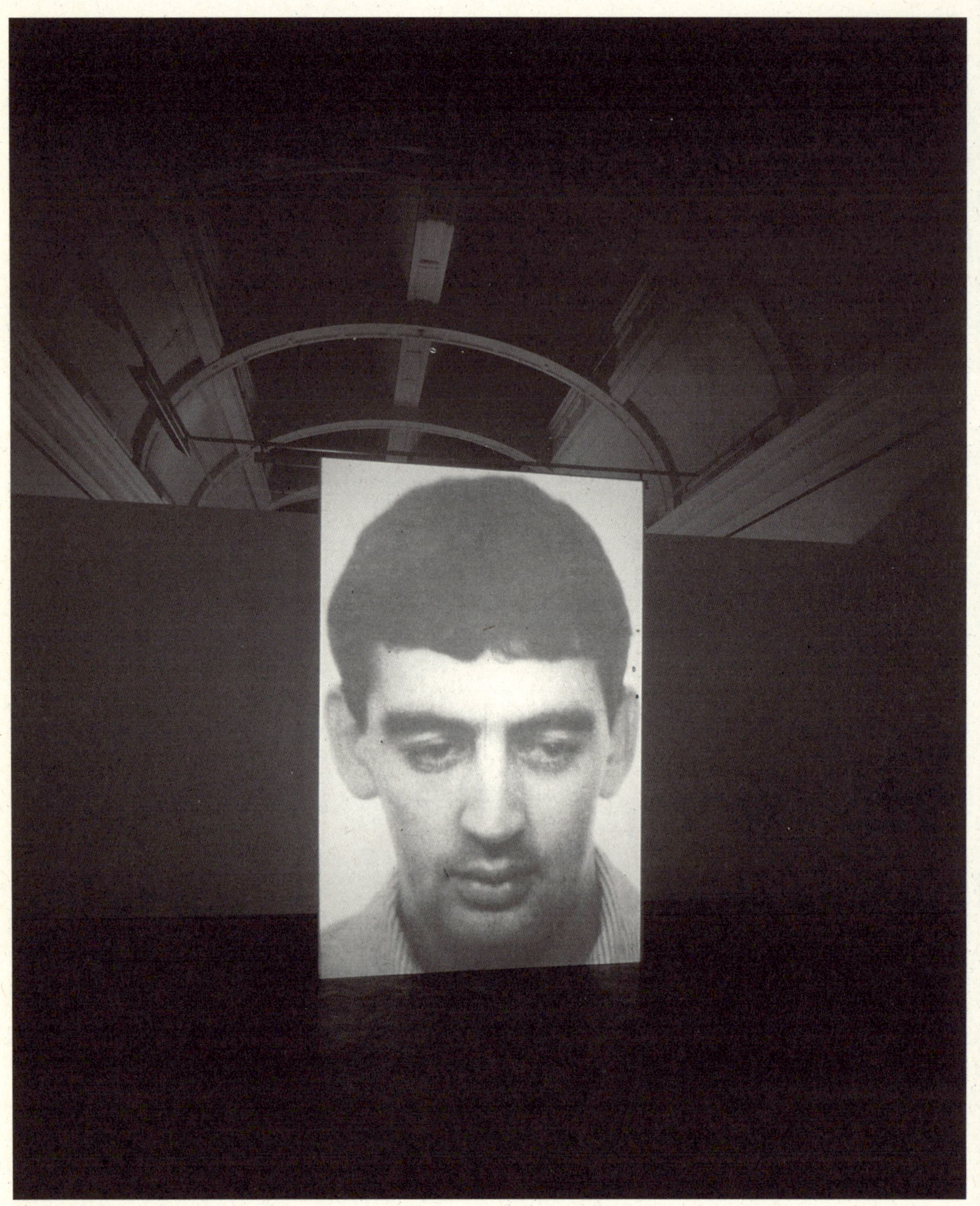

 WILLIE DOHERTY

They're all the same

The clean sweet air is interrupted only by the lingering aroma of turf smoke.
I'm pathetic.
The verdant borders of twisting lanes are splattered with blood red fuschia.
I'm barbaric.
Nowhere is the grass so green or so lush.
It's in my bones.
Nowhere are the purples and blues of the mountains so delicately tinged.
I am ruthless and cruel.
Nowhere is the sea so clear and calm and, with barely a moment's notice, the waves so dark and angry.
I am solid.
Nowhere has the sky such a range of delicate blues and mysterious greys.
I am essentially evil.
The sky is at its most dynamic in the West, where it is contrasted sharply against the white limestone walls.
I never saw such walls.
They represent the blood and sweat of countless generations. For all this land is 'made' land, hand made.
I am proud and dedicated.
For me, there is no alternative.
Upon seeing the grey barrenness of this limestone country one of Cromwell's generals complained
"there is not enough timber to hang a man, enough water to drown him, or enough earth to bury him."
I am uncivilised and uneducated.
On a clear day, when there is no haze to obscure the view, it is possible to gaze across the open landscape.
I have its history in my bones and on my tongue.
It's written all over my face.
Rain or shine, there are few landscapes whose colour, scale and contrast impress so immediately.
I'm crazy.
Nowhere are the nights so dark.
So dark that you cannot see the end of the road.
I'm innocent.
I'm cynical.
Nowhere is the sand on the beaches so fine and white.
I am patient. I have a vision.
Smooth, age-worn stones wet with rain.
Even the rain is different there.
The soft Atlantic rain which often seems to cover the whole country adds depth and subtlety to its colour.
I am dignified.
The clean sweet air is interrupted only by the lingering aroma of turf smoke.
I'm pathetic.
The verdant borders of twisting lanes are splattered with blood red fuschia.
I'm barbaric.
Nowhere is the grass so green or so lush.
I am decent and truthful.
It's in my bones.
Nowhere is the sea so clear and calm and, with barely a moment's notice, the waves so dark and angry.
I am solid.
Nowhere has the sky such a range of delicate blues and mysterious greys.
I am essentially evil.
The sky is at its most dynamic in the West, where it is contrasted sharply against the white limestone walls.
I never saw such walls.
They represent the blood and sweat of countless generations. For all this land is 'made' land, hand made.
I am proud and dedicated...

Douglas Gordon

Attraction — Repulsion *Interview by Stéphanie Moisdon*

Stéphanie Moisdon If one tried to establish a link between your different pieces, a narrative link which would directly connect your early work with your latest pieces, I would say briefly that your research is more based on an examination of perception than of representation and that it veers more towards inscription/writing (almost retinian) than towards types of reading and interpretation.

Douglas Gordon I kind of like the idea that the work seems more like an inscription rather than an interpretation, insofar as this relates directly to the pieces I was making before using film and video. I had been involved in performance work and quite large scale installations, but when I was based in London (between '88-'90) there was a literal problem with the amount of space I had available to work with. I got more interested in manipulating a certain space using only text (I should say that this was pretty much a pragmatic decision, to begin with). Eventually I felt that I wanted to work much less with the idea of 'site-specificity' and much more by engaging in the ambiguities of the 'psychological space'.

Around this time I went back to live in Glasgow and one of the first exhibitions I was involved with was *Self Conscious State* at the 3rd Eye Centre. It seemed important to me that I should try and make something more than the usual kind of smart-ass specific work that was all over the place at that time.

In any case, I felt as if I knew too much about the city, or the situations. I couldn't just skim the surface and make some comments and then fly off to somewhere else to do the same thing all over again. So, it was this fact of knowing too much that interested me and I tried to use this in the work *List of Names*. The work was trying to examine our system of cognition and memory very much with the idea that Roland Barthes talks about when he mentions photography and punctum. So, for this work, I tried to remember everyone that I had met and simply display all of these

names in the gallery. There were 1440 names
at that time, and the work is ongoing. It
functioned quite honestly and as much as
possible as a mirror of the actual mechanism
of memory that most of us use all the time.
This meant that on the one hand the system
was impressively large, and on the other hand
it was unbearably oppressive. It was an
accurate and honest statement but it was full
of small mistakes (like forgetting the names
of some friends etc…), so there were some
embarrassing elements in the work, but that
all seemed to be quite close to the truth of
how our head functions anyway. Sometimes
it works and sometimes it doesn't.

Moisdon This is apparent in your latest
works. There is a direct correlation with
neuro-psychological phenomena, linked to
memory and its temporal quality and its
malfunction.

Gordon Yes, I was specifically interested in
the collapse of this system precisely because
it's an aspect of life that most of us don't want
to acknowledge and certainly don't want to
happen (for basic survival instincts). I made a
small group of wall drawings about 3 states of
amnesia: 'I have forgotten everything', 'I
cannot remember anything' and 'I remember
nothing'. Now, these drawings should have
made no sense to anyone because all of the
words were spread all over the place,
repeated, and in different sizes. Logically, if
we can use that word, they should not make
any sense. But everyone who saw these
drawings could read them immediately, in
contradiction to what they might have
thought. It could be seen as if one's
knowledge of how to read was inescapable —
as if one could be a slave to this mechanism
of legibility, word construction, and meaning.

So, for me the system was imploding again,
and I enjoyed this contradiction and
confusion.

Working with this kind of ideas led me to
think of playing a lot more with the
possibilities of construction and dysfunction
in a pyschological space. And I should
emphasise the playing aspect, because quite
often the work is discussed as a game to be
played out by the viewer.

My interest in film and video, and specifically
cinema, is closely related to this
preoccupation with memory. It is surely the
case that every human being is interested in
neuro-psychological phenomena because,
statistically, almost every family has had, or
will have, some experience of disfunctional
behaviour. So, it's something we live with. We
can be fascinated by this subject and we can
be terrified of it.

So for me, fear and repulsion and fascination
are critical elements in both the world of this
science and the world of cinema. We can be
attracted to the spectacle of cinema while
watching something completely repulsive.
This is clear if you see some of the archive
medical footage that I have used in *10 ms⁻¹* or
Hysterical or the installation at the Van
Abbemuseum. There is a real problem here,
of how one is supposed to look at these
images. Firstly, we don't know where to locate
the image, in terms of a context. This could
be Hollywood, but this could also be real. And
the medium is film and video, but it's not a
cinema, and it's not presented as something
to be sat in front of and watched. Perhaps
there is a narrative, but perhaps not. How
long are viewers prepared to watch
something before they can decide what it is
that they are watching? It's also not an image

which has been constructed by the artist, so what are these images doing here and why are we looking at them? And if one does look at the images then you have to walk around them; you see that what is happening on screen might be quite painful — both physically and psychologically — but it has a seductive surface. What do you do — switch off or face the possibility that a certain sadistic mechanism may be at work? I think that by reappropriating these images, and collapsing the system that they are associated with, then the confusion can be quite interesting.

Moisdon In *24 Hour Psycho, Unpredictable incidents…, Hysterical* and so on, whether it be a question of real life experiences, snippets of text, films, or archives, your work virtually always undergoes the same kind of process. This process resembles an abduction or the taking of hostages (with the consent of the victim varying each time). What is it about this act of possession or appropriation that strikes you as relevant or important?

Gordon It's a strange idea. I've never thought of appropriation as abduction. But the suggestion that a hostage might have some degree of consent is interesting and dangerous at the same time. It makes me think of all the controversy around Patty Hearst. I remember reading those newspaper and magazine articles when I was really young. I always thought that her short life as a bank robber was much more exciting than a humdrum existence as some rich kid, so from my point of view, at that time, it seemed logical that she would have colluded with her captors.

And in referring back to these images that I have used, then, yes, there are some clear similarities with the kind of relationships that necessarily develop between a hostage and a captor, in the way that both become dependent on one another, for all sorts of reasons (food, heat, communication), but also, that they need one another, however temporarily, in order to identify themselves as human beings.

Moisdon And what about the films you use, in relation to this?

Gordon If you look at *24 Hour Psycho,* or *Unpredictable incidents…,* in particular, the hostage metaphor works quite well. Both the works are using high profile and popular media icons in order to 'extort' another role with those images. I think it's important, though, to say that these works, as I see it, are not simply works of appropriation. They are more like acts of affiliation. When I was wanting to use Hitchcock's *Psycho,* it wasn't a straightforward case of abduction. The original work is a masterpiece in its own right, and I've always loved to watch it. In many ways I did not want to change this situation, either for me or the other viewers. I wanted to maintain the authorship of Hitchcock so that when an audience saw my *24 Hour Psycho* they would think much more about Hitchcock and much less, or not at all about me. Also, when most people see *Unpredictable incidents…* they are not so conscious of the artist but spend time thinking and talking about their own memories of the original *Star Trek* series and how they watch television. So, in many ways, this again fits your analogy of the hostage and captor. The artist as a captor can be quite content to sit in the background, and if everything is running smoothly, they can play an anonymous role in the equation.

THOSE I DO NOT KNOW

THOSE I WILL NEVER KNOW

THOSE I HAVE

THOSE I WOULD NOT LIKE TO KNOW

THOSE I HAVE FORGOTTEN AND WIL

THOSE I WOULD LIKE TO KNOW

ORGOTTEN BUT WILL REMEMBER

THOSE I CAN NOT KNOW

NEVER REMEMBER

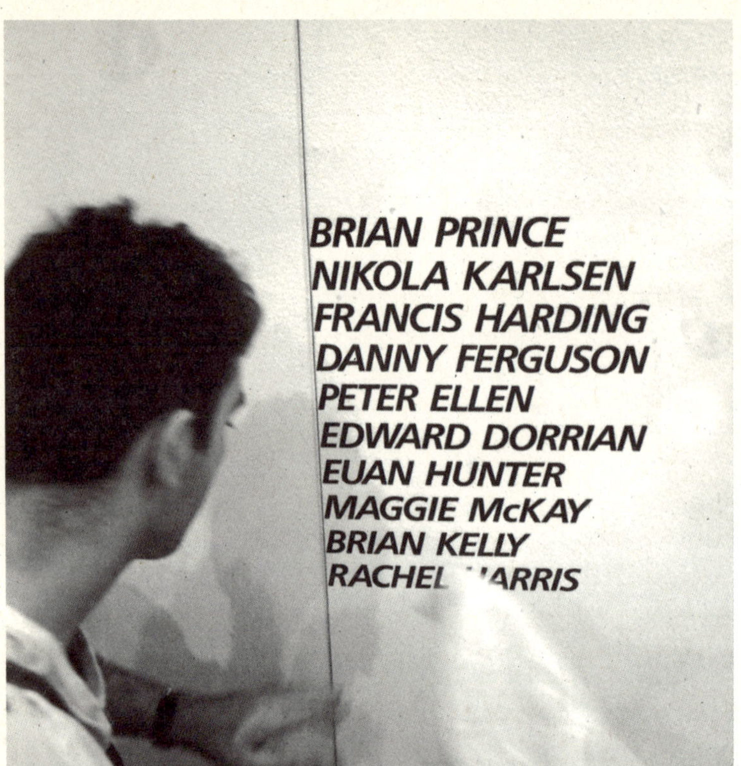
BRIAN PRINCE
NIKOLA KARLSEN
FRANCIS HARDING
DANNY FERGUSON
PETER ELLEN
EDWARD DORRIAN
EUAN HUNTER
MAGGIE McKAY
BRIAN KELLY 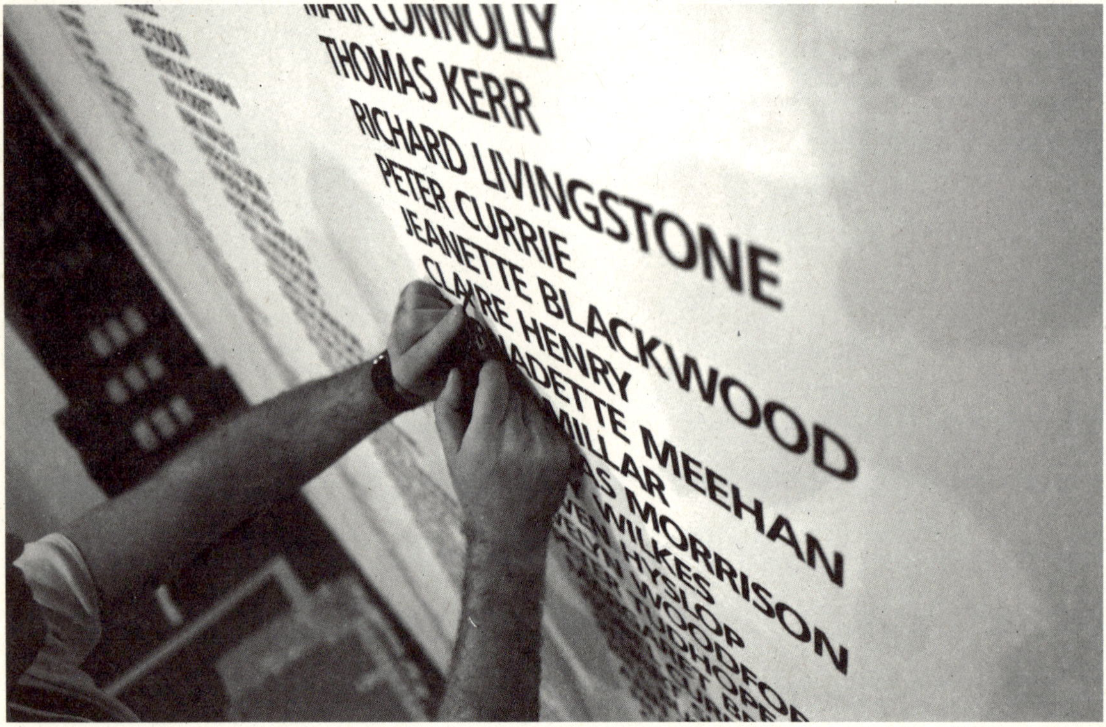
RACHEL HARRIS

MARK CONNOLLY
THOMAS KERR
RICHARD LIVINGSTONE
PETER CURRIE
JEANETTE BLACKWOOD
CLAIRE HENRY
BERNADETTE MEEHAN
MILLAR
MORRISON
WILKES
HYSLOP

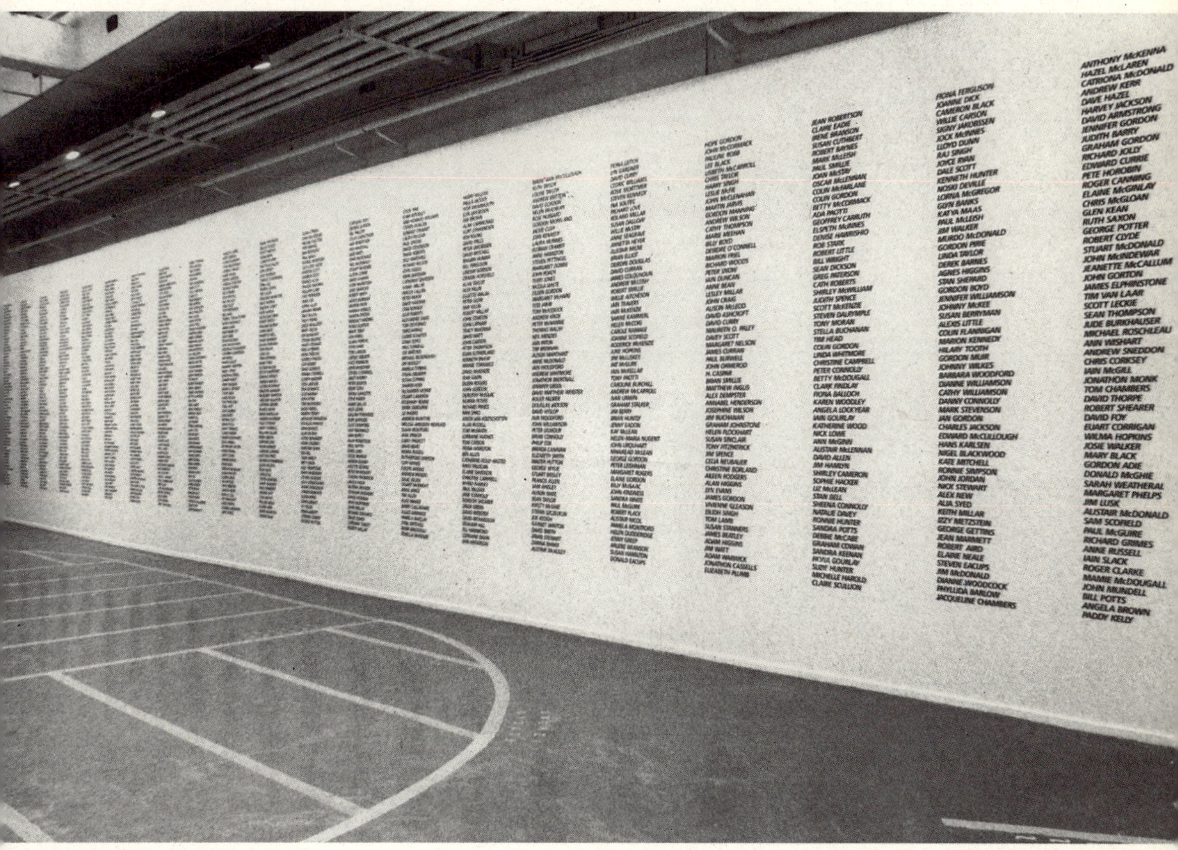

List with Names, 1990-ongoing
vinyl text
dimensions variable
courtesy Lisson Gallery, London

PAGE 58-59
Untitled, 1992
vinyl text
dimensions variable
collection Sadie Coles, London

A cheerful nihilist drinks orange juice and eats a brownie

Since the early nineties the Dutch artist Aernout Mik has caused a stir in the Netherlands and Belgium and recently in Germany with exhibitions of spatial works in which living creatures — human figures, dogs and hamsters —, semi-automatons, furniture and other household goods appear in a dramatically composed setting. Sometimes these scenes seemed to have been frozen in mid-action. The art lover could reconstruct the story on the spot from images created with the aid of photos, manipulated objects and things that looked like refuse. In other works Mik presented a tableau vivant in which people with an indeterminate identity carried out an act or were lost in thought. Certain activities were endlessly repeated, so that the whole seemed like an invocation of the dictatorship that controls our life unnoticed: the long list of rules and regulations which, to a greater degree than we realise, channel our individual behaviour within the social order into fixed courses.

These spatial artworks have the effect of a painting in which we see reflected the relation between people and objects or people and their surroundings, albeit exaggerated and distorted as in a hall of mirrors. This is why it would be incorrect to speak of installations. That term in no way covers their almost magical force. Mik's works can best be defined as phantasmagorias in which the dream intrudes into everyday reality. Sometimes they are distinctly amusing. But there is also something disturbing about them, because you have a sense of all kinds of dark forces lying beneath the surface. You realise that reality in Mik's images is not straightforward, even though you can see the things concretely in front of you, and you are sometimes very close to the people. This makes you muse spontaneously on existential questions. Is man the product of a history written without his knowledge? Can he really make contact with his surroundings, or have things turned away from him? To what extent does he need the intoxication to hold his ground out there in the heart-rending reality?

The work of Central European and Slav authors such as Franz Kafka, Witold Gombrowicz and Vladimir Nabokov has a similar existential charge. In language a grotesque outside world is depicted that dominates us and puts a heavy burden on the individual consciousness — so that we are in fact left with little recourse but to take refuge in an inner world. These writers describe so accurately how man gives substance to his earthly existence that the incongruities, conflicts and absurdities beneath the surface of the visible world are exposed. Something similar takes place in the work of Aernout Mik. His images are fragile: what appears to be an entity disintegrates before the eyes of the viewer. Mik's early photographic works have been compared with the picturesque images of Jeff Wall, but it has not been realised that Jeff Wall is making as it were a last attempt to hold things together. If you look at Mik's large, digitally produced photographic work *Für Nichts und wieder Nichts* (1992), you become aware of a huge gulf between the rugged, once rural setting, filled with the most banal junk of our age, and the young Asians who stand stock-still on that spot, staring into space and appearing to transcend above the earth's surface.

In the work of Aernout Mik serious subjects are always viewed from a light-hearted angle. The exhibition *Mommy, I am sorry* (De Vleeshal, Middelburg, 1995), which he created together with the New York architect Adam Kalkin, was an ode to homo ludens. It is problematic and perhaps indeed tragic that as a member of bourgeois society the individual is under pressure to give up his desires, imagination and spontaneity in order to achieve various prosaic goals. In *Mommy, I am sorry* saying goodbye to childhood was postponed; the title refers to the decision to put aside for a while, in a carnival of crazy events, the good manners carefully learnt. What actually happened at this exhibition cannot be summarised in a single sentence. In a house built in the entrance to the Vleeshal, with tar and discarded library books among other things, playful events took place according to a particular scenario for four weeks: two little girls, one of whom was dressed as a wasp, had a conversation about perfume; a Dutch chess master played simultaneous games against local residents; visitors were presented with biscuits; a soaking wet policeman supposedly sought shelter from the storm...

The solution Aernout Mik found for the problem of how to keep alive the memory of this kind of exhibition is characteristic of his view of how art is treated in our culture. Instead of a catalogue he devised a kind of music box. This *Mommy box,* which was produced in a limited edition, plays a tune when you turn a mechanism by hand; you can put one of the ten slides of the exhibition provided on a lit glass plate; there is a booklet with a short story, and on the inside the box smells of camphor. Of course the story told by the *Mommy box* is different from that told by the exhibition and that's exactly the point. What matters is the recurring question of how to take leave of the past in the right way. The essential thing is how to construct a memory that is meaningful in the present. From this point of view the accumulation of artefacts in museums, which seems to continue automatically, is problematic, because all too often there is a lack of the imagination required to again give the objects something of the life they once reflected.

Although Aernout Mik occupies a position of his own, his work shows certain elements that can be understood on the basis of general developments in art. The eighties were characterised by aesthetic detachment, a specific fetishism and the seemingly universally accepted diktat of perfect form. In the nineties a generation of young artists rebelled against this. The result was a veritable explosion of the object. From 1990 on we saw how the artwork as 'Gestalt' was pushed aside by all kinds of context-sensitive interventions, 'trash art' and exhibitions in which the emphasis was on processes of change. Nonetheless, it is time to realise that there is a big difference between someone like Paul Valéry, who with his fine maxim "what is finished, has not been made" meant to say that artistic achievements should reflect thinking that perseveres through the whole creative process, and the misapprehensions about the meaning of process now prevailing, as painfully evident in exhibitions where in a primitive gesture the complete interior of the artist's studio is displayed in public. Mik certainly is interested in the potential of the process in art. But the variations in his works with live extras are always ruled by a strict score, so that each snapshot of a phased action is clearly conveyed. In a sense the moment in its inexplicability is more important to Mik than the narrative suggestion implicit in an action that takes place in time. Unlike in literature, theatre or film, we see here that each moment contains an entire drama, because all the signs are present of a story that refers to past and future. This is clearly seen when we look closely at the world in which we live. But the question is what do you do with that insight. I have a young friend, Eleonora, who visits me from time to time. She is always hungry. In less than two hours she devours Italian biscuits, cheese sandwiches, pieces of apple, fruit juice, liquorice all sorts, etc. Meantime she plays chess, looks at picture books and draws. A regular feature of her repertoire consists of working the *Mommy box;* without that ritual her visit is not complete. For Eleonora, I imagine, the music is the promise of something special awaiting her. Whereas it reminds me of something that will never return.

Mark Kremer

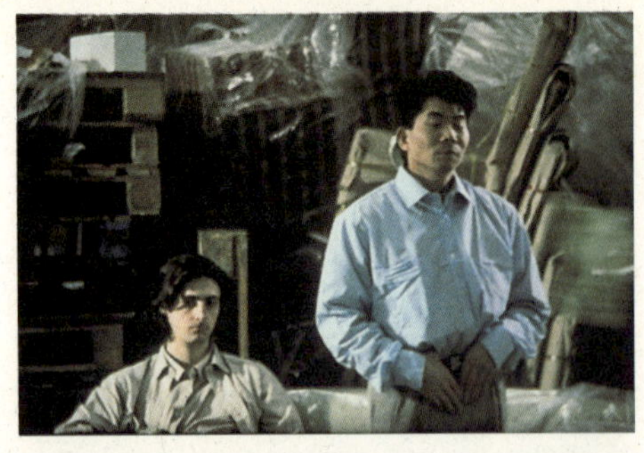

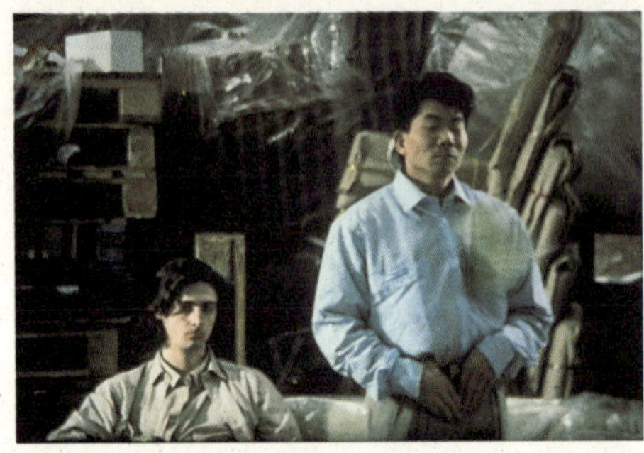

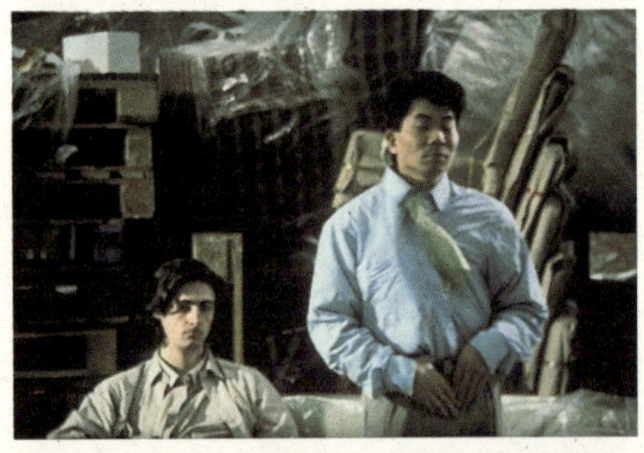

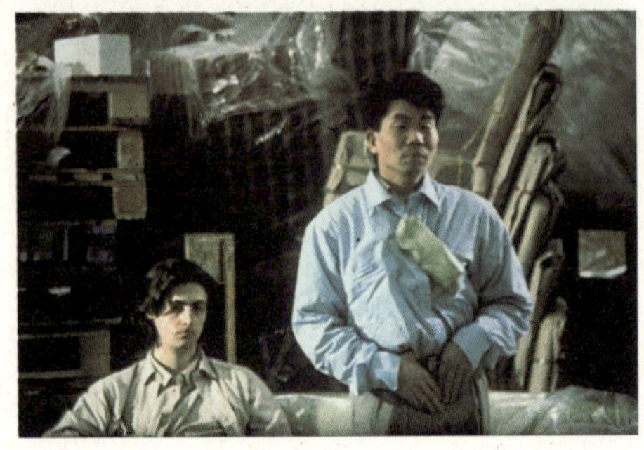

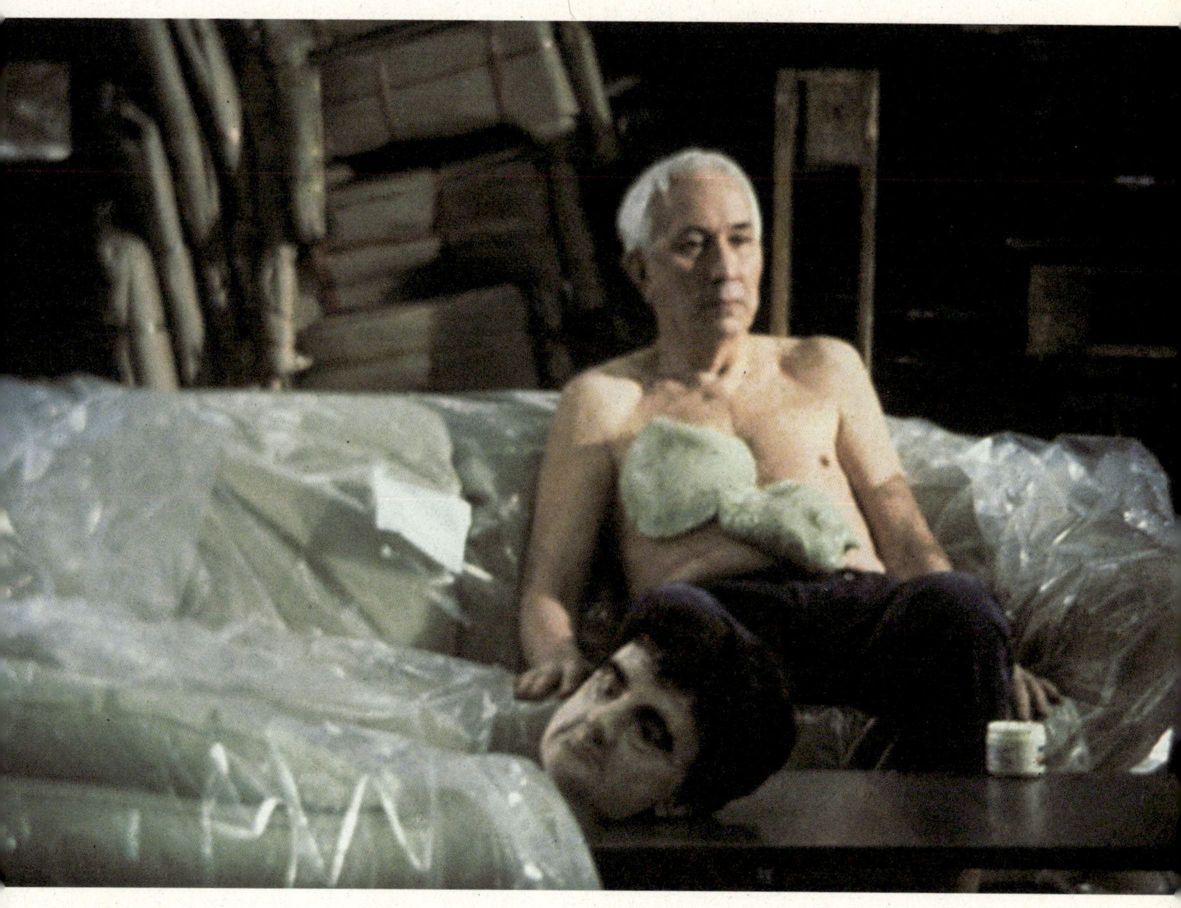

Fluff, 1996
S-16 mm film on video
video installation
camera: Marjoleine Boonstra

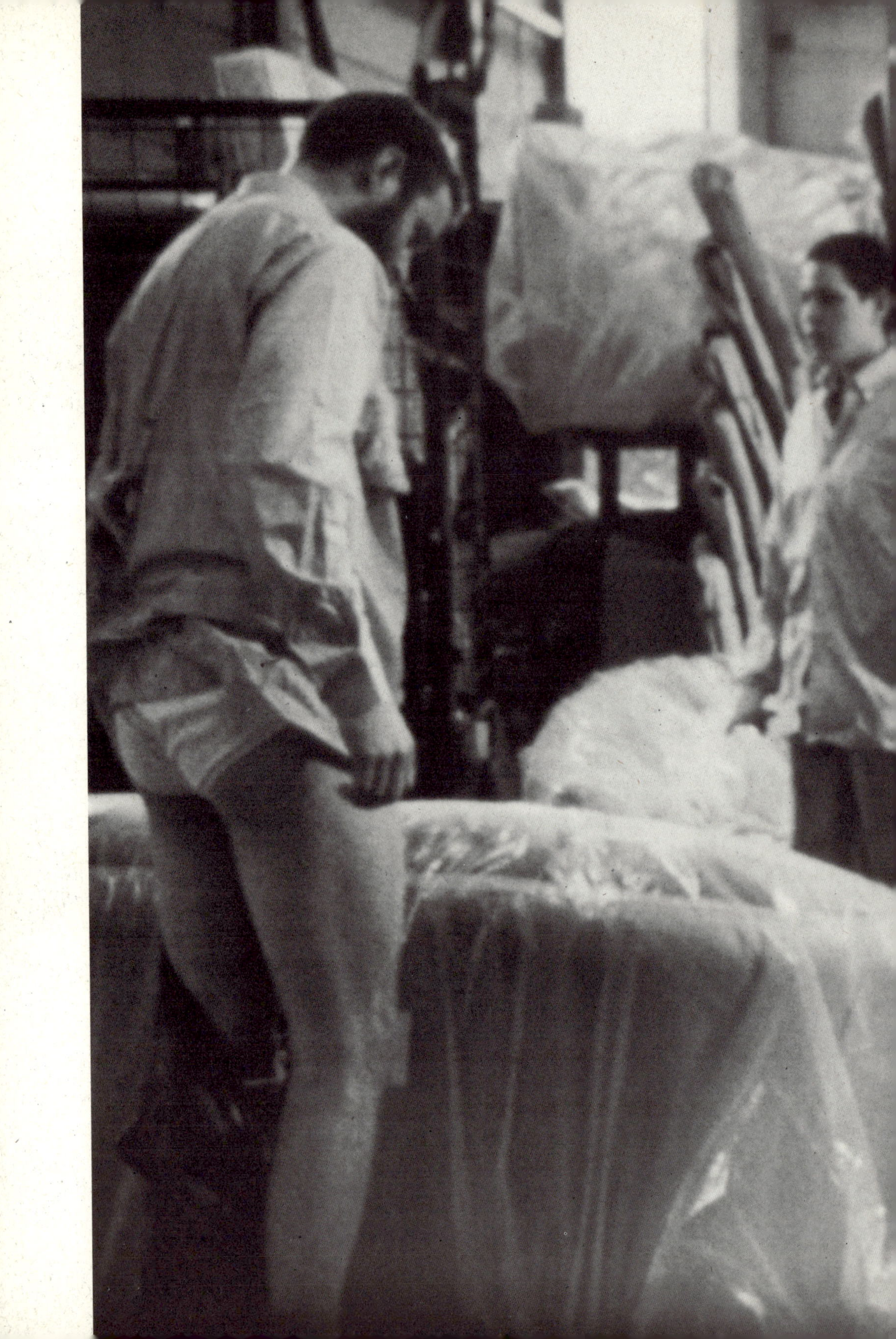

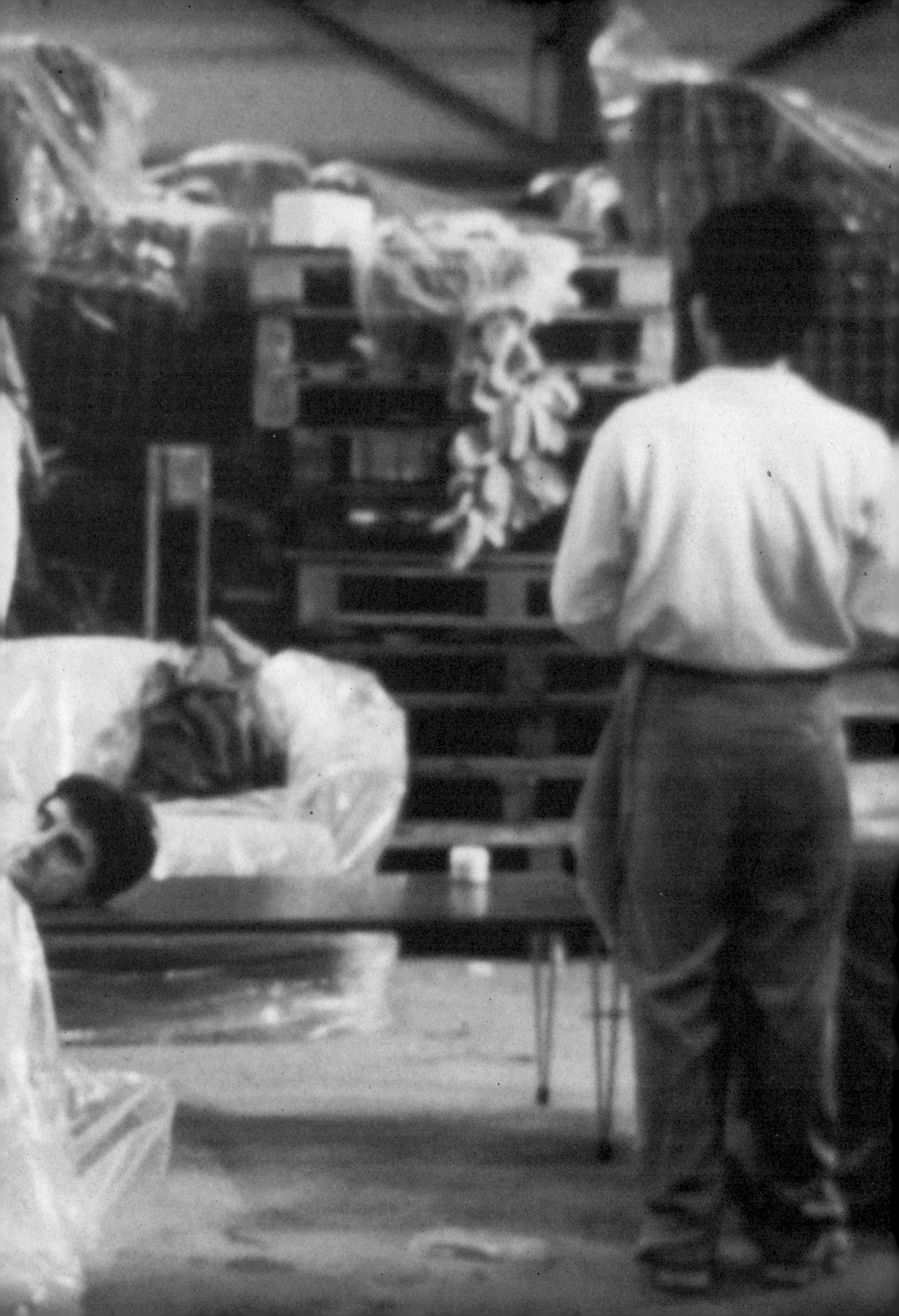

Alters

"...video's real medium is a psychological situation, the very terms of which are to withdraw attention from an external object — an Other — and invest it in the Self", wrote Rosalind Krauss in a pioneering study of seventies video.[1] Basing her analysis on a series of single channel video tapes, she argued that the video apparatus functioned as a mirror, and that the works of art it generated served as records of this technologically mediated narcissistic encounter. Describing that mode of seventies' practice as 'intrasubjective', David Joselit has identified an alternate yet concurrent mode, based in video installation, which he designates 'intersubjective'.[2] Instancing installations by Dan Graham and Peter Campus which also incorporated instant feedback, Joselit contends that this second strand of video art was engaged in a psychological self-encounter constructed in and by social space. These two modes of narcissism suggest, he concludes, "the continuum along which video practice has long been charted: on the one hand as a privatized exploration of the self, and on the other as a remapping of the discursive formations of the mass media".[3]

Tony Oursler's recent video projections imbricate these two strands in a re-probing of the implications of the medium's novel capacity for instant feedback, weaving them together with the tropes of mass-media pop-psychologizing. While he, too, attributes metaphorical power to that technological innovation, Oursler dispenses with the technique itself, though he still keeps the projected image hostage to its source; he also relinquishes the monitor, which the two earlier theoretical models had used both as a vehicle and as the literal site of encounter. Replacing the immaterial transmission of the screen with a projection in real space, Oursler not only makes these embodiments incarnate but posits as integral to such self-encounters a disturbing, fantasmatic actuality.

Since 1992 Oursler has been employing mannikins — dolls and puppets — onto whose heads he projects faces. Emoting at the least, but, more often, narrating at length, these figures whine, wail, threaten, complain, and cajole relentlessly, indifferent to the presence, or absence, of anyone else. Prisoners of various predicaments, their physical circumstances, manifestations or exacerbations of their mental disorders, they heedlessly pour forth their litanies of woe into the darkened gallery spaces. In *Get Away #2* (1994) the figure lies prone, staring balefully from beneath the corner of a mattress which pinions it to the ground; by contrast, the 'alter' of *Judy* (1994) cowers underneath a sofa, one side of which has been propped up to create a temporary, makeshift shelter. *White Trash/Phobic*

(1993) presents its dual overlapping psyches as protagonists who engage in an abstract conversation, while wedged in opposing corners of a room. Others are crammed into, or alternately, take refuge in giant empty pill capsules, the possible sources of their delirious ravings.

The term Oursler prefers for these dummies, these spectral manifestations, is effigy. While the word may be a synonym for a sculptured likeness, it also has a more specific meaning, one that catches the dark undertones ever present in his art: "a crude figure often in the form of a stuffed dummy that is tortured or disposed of (often by burning or by hanging) to represent treatment felt to be due to a person who is the object of hatred".[4] From golems to voodoo dolls, effigies thus have manifold affiliates that are similarly the repositories of malevolent projections or repressed desires, cravings and fantasies.
Staring back at the beams of light illuminating them, Oursler's projected figures seem transfixed by the very sources of their being. The transference of the physiognomy from the depthless screen of the monitor to the discombobulated body of a mannikin enacts metaphorically that externalising of the self or part-self that characterises dissociations of the psyche; that is, it mirrors that unconscious defence mechanism in which a set of mental activities is split off from the mainstream of consciousness to function as a separate unit. Irrespective of whether they are identified as hysterical, phobic, obsessive, manic, paranoic, depressive or psychotic his spectral characters exhibit the uni-dimensional persona of the crazed or possessed. Narcissistically fixated by the glare that animates them, they take on hallucinatory appearances reminiscent of phantoms, poltergeists, grotesques and ghouls — the archetypal protagonists not only of nightmares but of the modern genres of horror and their timeless predecessors, folk-tales, all sanctioned collective repositories for the repressed and the suppressed. In addition to supplementing these traditional arenas for figuring psychoses and neuroses, today's mass media welcomes novel variants in the guise of docudramas and tabloid scoops that feature multiple personality disorders and their affiliates. Oursler's eerie dummies partake equally of all these realms. Temporarily relinquishing video, over the past few months Oursler has made several works which, while retaining his signature low-tech means and make-shift fabrication, now allude to the rapidly evolving media of computer based technologies. Reduced to a bare electric bulb paired with a synchronized sound track, this series no longer addresses the psychopathologies of the self but the very basis of identity of any subject. In *Talking Light* (1996) for example, a voice intermittently bursts forth, in concert with the flicker of the bulb illuminating the blackness. Divested of all corporeality and condemned to repeating its tedious monologue in an undefined and indefinite space, this disembodied speaker

comes one stage closer to annihilation than the truncated organs kept alive in jars of a formeldahyde-like substance, found in *Submerged* (1995/6) and related works. The possession of a body and hence the capacity to situate itself physically in space is a prerequisite not only of a subject being able to take up a position, but the very condition of a coherent identity. In certain psychotic states, notably psychasthenia, subjectivity is no longer anchored in the body, since the body and subject fail to mesh. Such psychootics both lose their perspective on the world and cease to be a source of perception for space itself captivates and replaces them. This results, according to theorist Elizabeth Grosz in the primacy of the subject's own perspective being "replaced by the gaze of another for whom the subject is merely a point in space, not the focal point organising space".5

Talking Light (1996) might be read as a wry reprise of Samuel Beckett's famous protagonist from *Not I,* which also spews its fractured monologue in a dimensionless world. Beckett's sparely embodied subject — nothing but a silhouetted mouth — like Oursler's, displaces its identity (in this case from the first to the third person, 'she'), yet its laconic utterances convey an unexpected resilience, a surprising irrepressibility. By contrast, *Talking Light*'s wan stutterer, devoid of all forms of dissociation, of all externalising, lacks not only the possibility of self-encounter but even a self-sustaining if deprecatory humor. Split off from its physical body and hence deprived of spatial co-ordinates, this spark of consciousness, this blip in a limitless and liminal void, offers a sly yet incisive critique of the immaterial subjects deemed unique to cyberspace. The avatars of cyberspace identities extoll the freedoms that stem from the transparency, dispensability and redundancy of the body — mere 'meat' — yet for Grosz and other sceptical critics such conditions both create a radically flawed subject, and are inimical to the task of self-consolidation or self-reconstruction. Indeed, as *Talking Light* attests, they closely approximate the symptoms of certain psychoses. If this bleak work is prophetic of his future forays, for Oursler the virtual worlds of electronic and cyberspace are unlikely to prove any more reassuring or reaffirming than the tragicomic universe overrun with phantom representations that is his vision of our everyday, phenomenal world.

Lynne Cooke

1. Rosalind Krauss, 'Video: The Aesthetics of Narcissism', *October 1,* Spring, 1976, p. 57.

2. David Joselit, *Film and Video Installation in the Biennale of Sydney,* unpublished paper, 1996.

3. ibid.

4. *Webster's Third New International Dictionary,* 1986.

5. Elizabeth Grosz, 'Lived Spatiality: Insect Space/Virtual Sex', *Agenda* 26-27, November/December and January/February, 1992-3, p. 7.

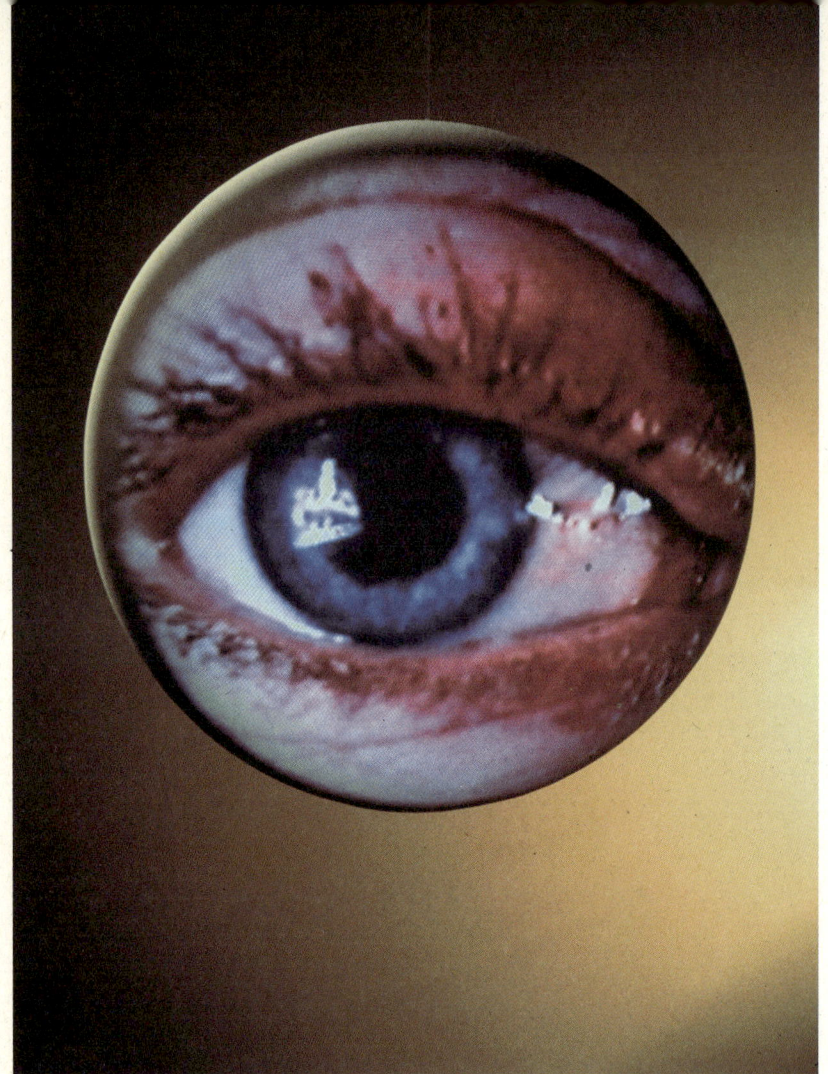

Fire, 1996
acrylic on fiber glass, VCR, video projector
diameter of sphere: 46 cm
performed by: Constance Dejong
courtesy Metro Pictures, New York

Crying, 1996
acrylic on fiber glass, VCR, video projector
diameter of sphere: 46 cm
performed by: Tracey Leipold
courtesy Metro Pictures, New York

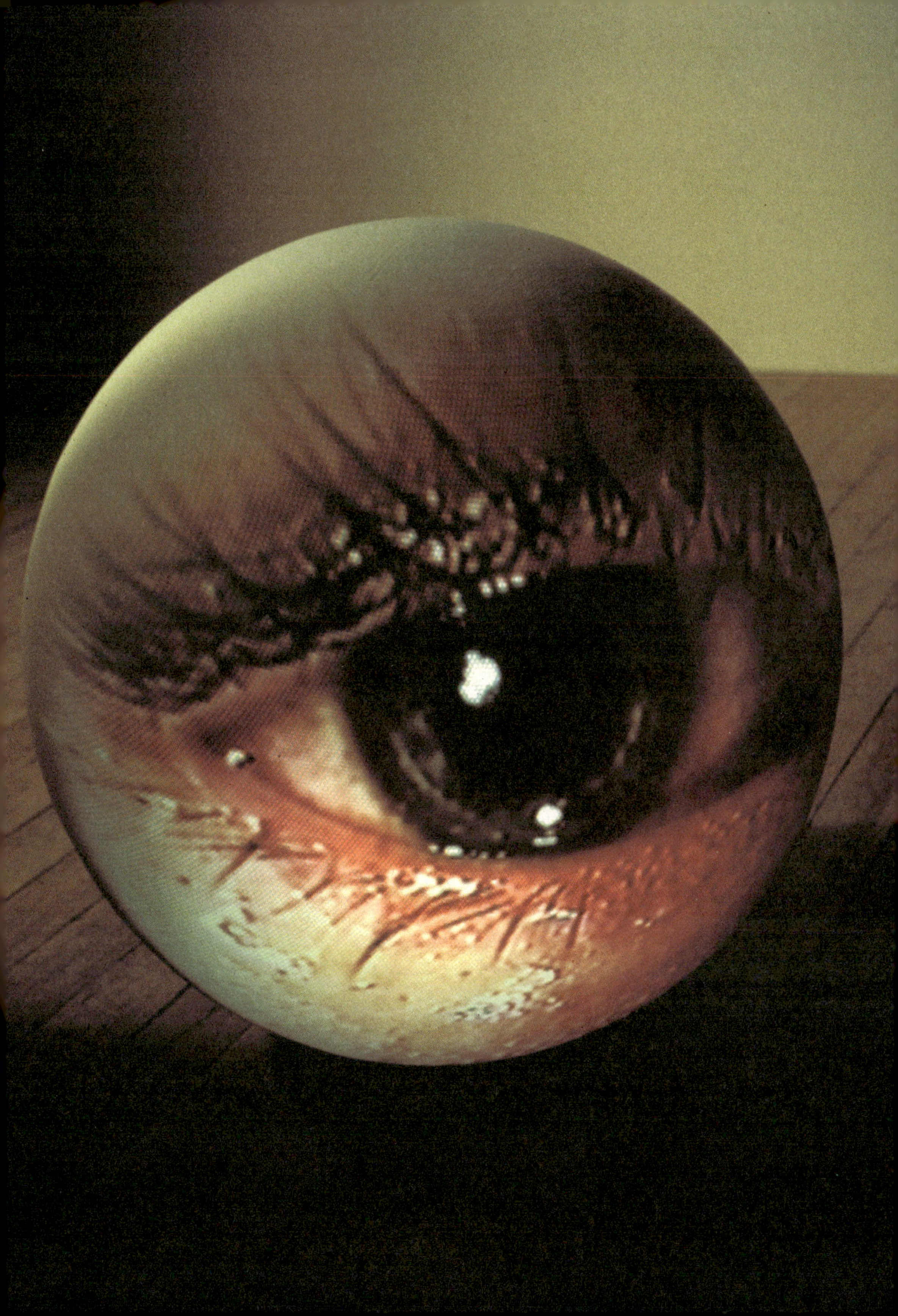

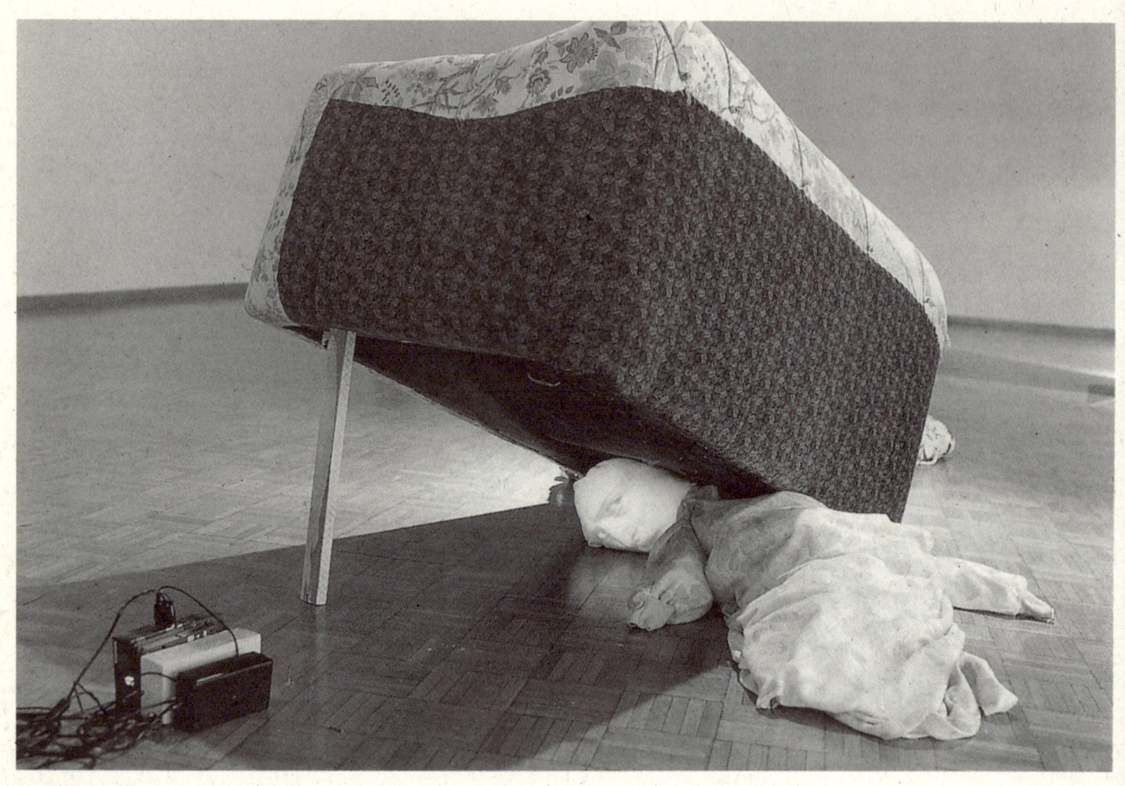

Judy,
1994 (detail)
installation
mixed media
courtesy Metro Pictures, New York

Autochthonous Alien, 1995
videoprojection on two dolls
doll (man) 206 x 33 x 33 cm
doll (woman) 199 x 33 x 33 cm
collection Stedelijk Van Abbemuseum, Eindhoven

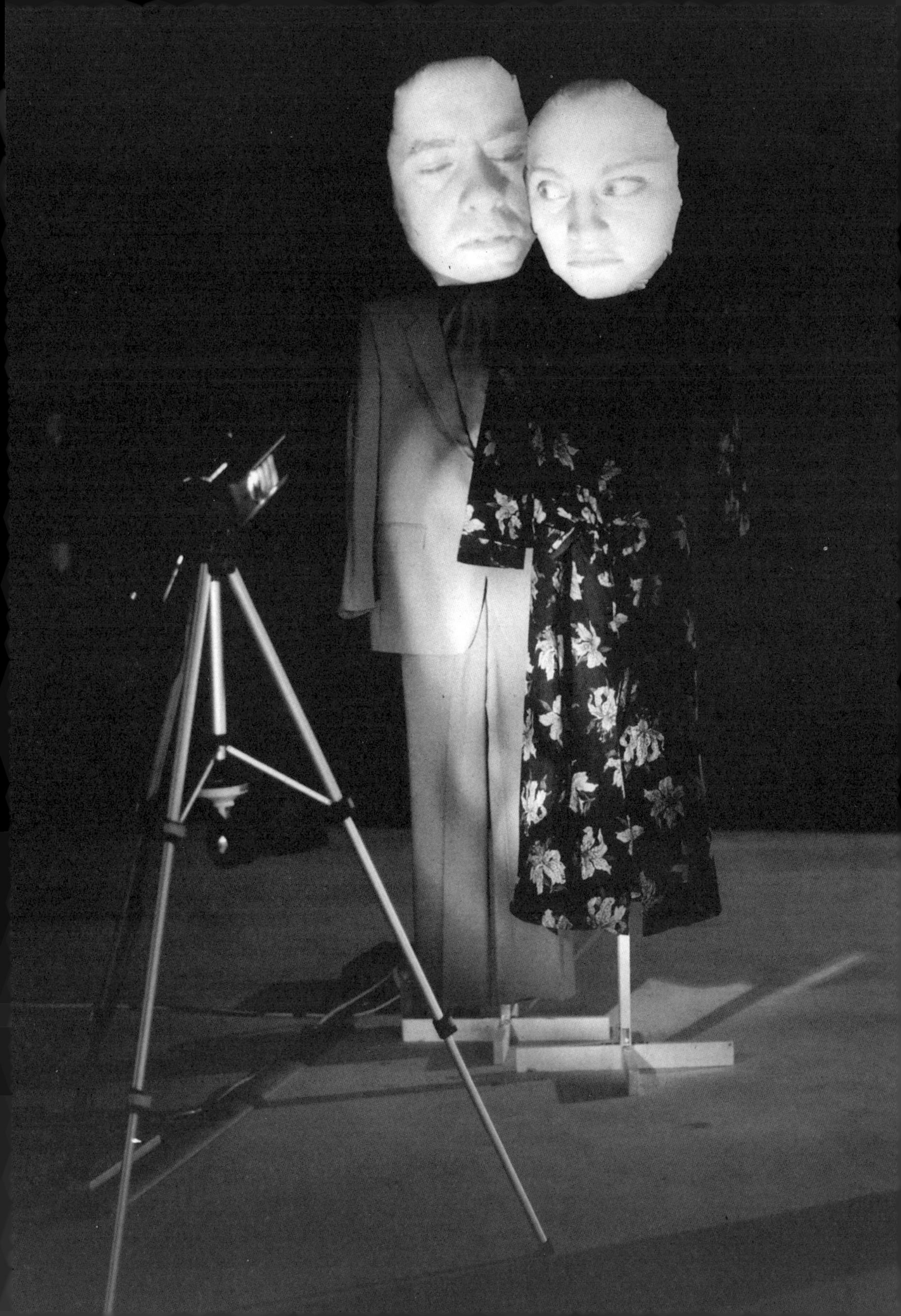

Anonymous

The beginning
Sam Samore produced his first pictures ten or eleven years ago. He called them
Situations (1980's). He operated just like a film director. This involved the ritual of
hiring photographers and instructing them: "Go out and photograph as many
different kinds of people, situations, age groups, genders, ethnicities as possible."
He was conceptually unspecific. He did not want to know anything about the
protagonists or the occasion of their meeting. So there was a loss of actual
narrative. Viewers, and this included Samore, had to make the synopsis up
themselves. The recurring minimalistic mood of these images was alive, vibrant,
exciting, mysterious.

The black and white thing
At the age of twelve Samore looked at a lot of late-night horror movies like
Frankenstein and *Dracula*. They were always in black and white. He didn't have a
colour TV like everybody else on the block.

The shift
After collecting the photographs Samore spent years looking at them. In a long
and fluctuating process he kept browsing through them, reaching back to them.
He still finds new pictures in his archives. Yet five years ago, when he was living

in Paris, he was amused by posing in the role of the photographer himself. Sam Samore once studied behaviourist psychology at the University of Wisconsin. He loves the frenzy of the methodological experiment. Would the pictures look different if he pushed the button? They didn't. But it is a good idea to change your myth once in a while. The new series of feverish and blurred images was called *Allegories of Beauty (Incomplete)*. His cinematographic eye lingers on the face and on delicious body fragments like nose, eyebrow, mouth, nape of neck and ear. The women and men dissolve almost ethereally in the coarse black and white grain, but without ever losing their physical presence.

The not completed

The *Allegories of Beauty (Incomplete)* remain in a permanent state of flux. Samore flirts with the word incomplete. He has used this term for other series, like the *Descriptions (Incomplete)*. The research stays eternally alive and cultivates an open discourse. It's about asking questions and exploring rather than providing answers. Clement Greenberg says that all great art is ugly. I wonder if Samore is trying to bring back the delightful beauty of Renaissance painting?

The beautiful

At the time of Socrates, or at least of the Kouros, the beautiful man was more important than the beautiful woman. Beauty was defined by the male body. The issues of beauty are complicated. Its subversive, frivolous pose lies beyond the singular appearance. With Samore's pictures we can imagine titles like *Beauty and the Beast*. Or *The Ugly Ducking*, because Sam Samore is a writer of fairy tales. He doesn't give any titles himself. When referring to a specific picture you have to describe it in your own words to the person you are speaking with.

The operational code

Three performative operations are involved in *Allegories of Beauty*, although they are not distinguished. One is the so-called document, one is the staging and one is the collage. Samore never uses the computer. He does it the so-called old-fashioned way.

The poems and the songs

One of Samore's obsessions is to write poems and songs for the windows of buildings, churches, boutiques, offices, restaurants, railway stations, museums, airports and the like, even buses. For the september 1996 exhibition called *Shopping* curated by Jérôme Sans, he created a sort of free flowing poetic verse for the windows of a cosmetic store, Face Stockholm, located in the notorious Soho district of New York City: *Climbing into the Source*. Samore departs within the

feverish rituals of beauty, desire and fantasy while simultaneously flashing in on
their respective correlative mode of being. His powerful fragmented phrases are
allegories for passing through the looking glass, exploring the vital world of
sophistication. Samore's song lyrics float lightly on the boutiques' architectural
skin and orifices, metaphorically personifying its function. The shop is deploted
as the place for the transformation of self, by way of body and mind.

The myth
Samore is a true fabulist. He makes up everything and seduces his potential
reader with unexpected weaves of sharp, dripping, cutting phrases. His first book
of fairy tales was published in 1994: *Tangled Web of Erotic Savage Cunning*. The
hypertext of his deconstruction of the uncanny is posthumanism. His second
book has just been completed: *Sumptuous Fire of the Stars* — it will melt behind
your gritting teeth.

The latest
In November of 1996 Samore introduced a new series of photographs, the
Scenario's (1990's). Things are different here. The mise-en-scène is precisely
staged and shot by Samore. For the very first time the distinction is made clear.
Real actors are carefully selected to perform under Samore's cool and knowing
directions. The ultimate transgression of these frivolous and ambiguous pictures
focuses on the symbolic as well as the imaginary. Think of Lancan's dialectic of
the eye and the gaze. In everything we look at. There is always a point from where
the picture is looking back at us, where we are already inscribed in the picture.

Michelle Nicol

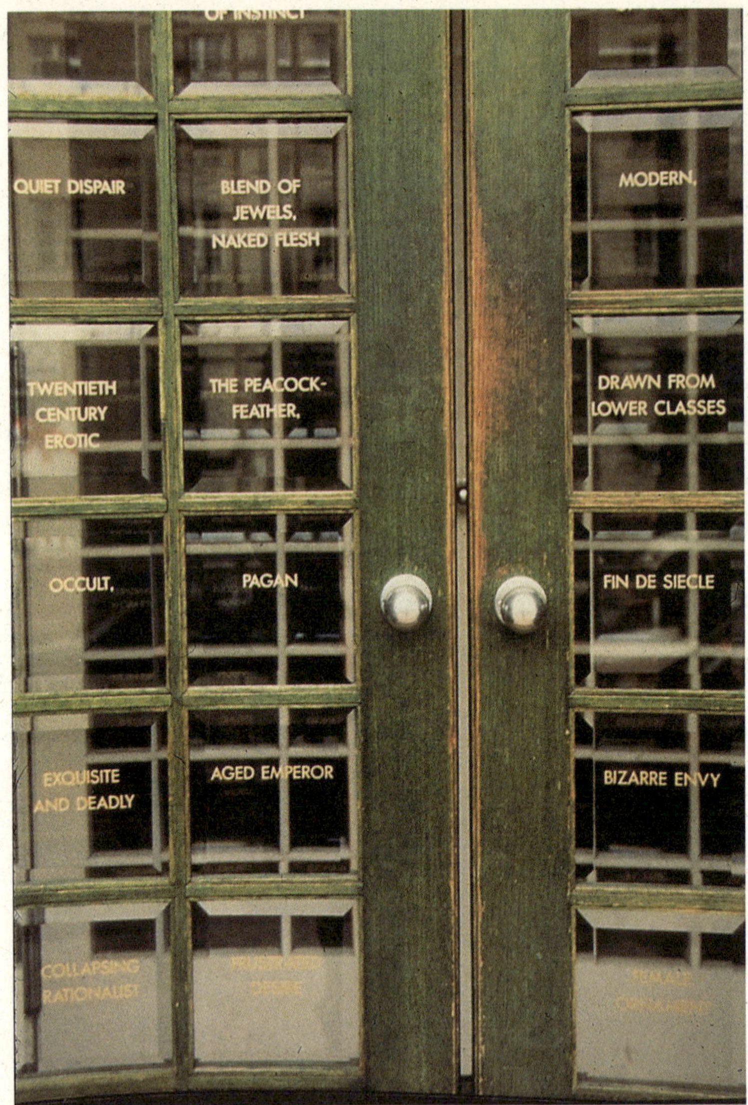

Gates of Heaven/Hell, 1993
Poem/song for the entrance doors of the Wiener Secession, Vienna. For a group exhibition curated by Jérôme Sans, called 'Viennese Story'.
gold vinyl letters on 300 windows
courtesy Wiener Secession, Vienna

Climbing into the Source, 1996
Poem/song for the windows of 'Face Stockholm', a cosmetic boutique in New York City. For a group exhibition curated by Jérôme Sans, called 'Shopping'.
citron yellow vinyl letters on 5 windows
courtesy Deitch Projects, New York

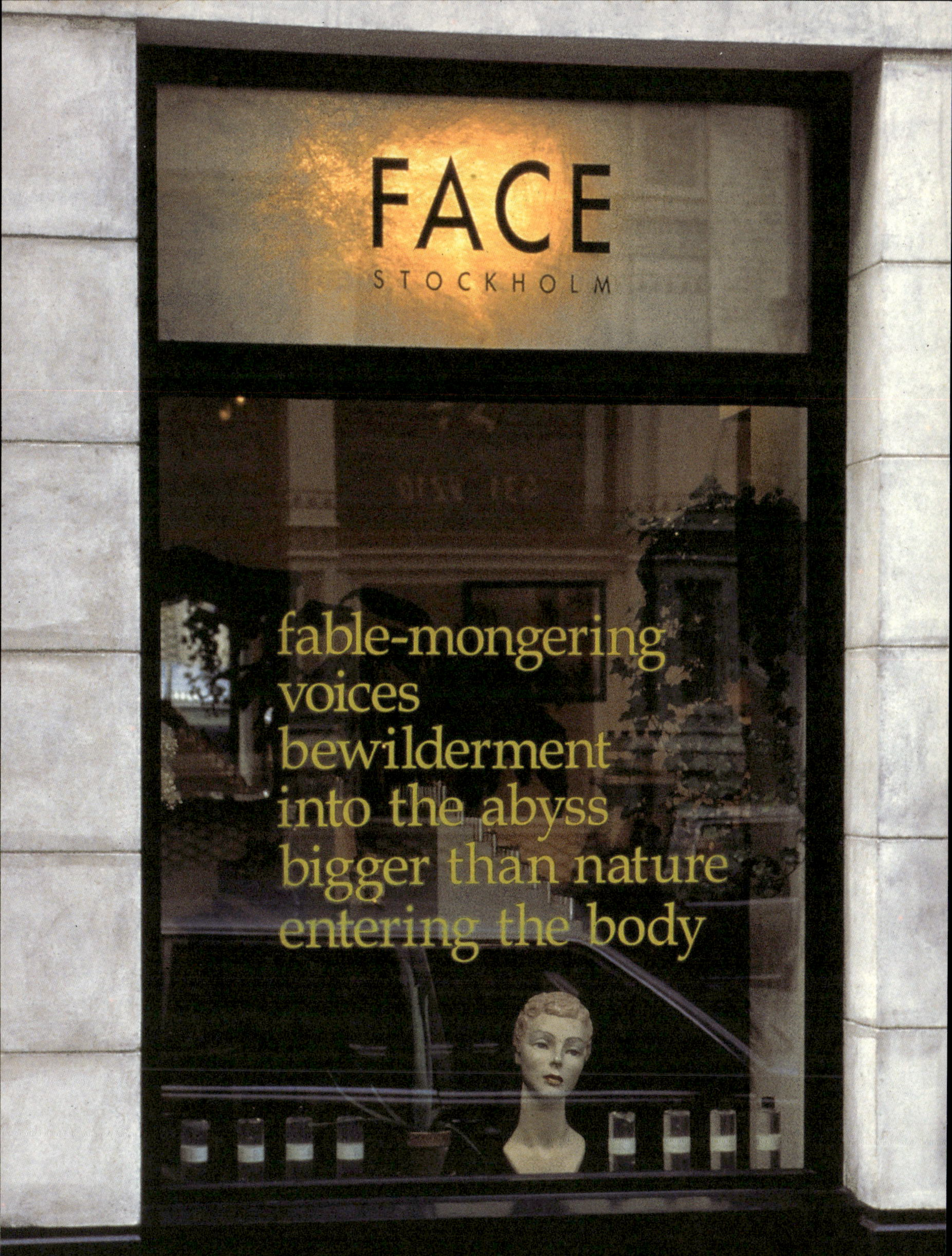

FACE
STOCKHOLM
fable-mongering
voices
bewilderment
into the abyss
bigger than nature
entering the body

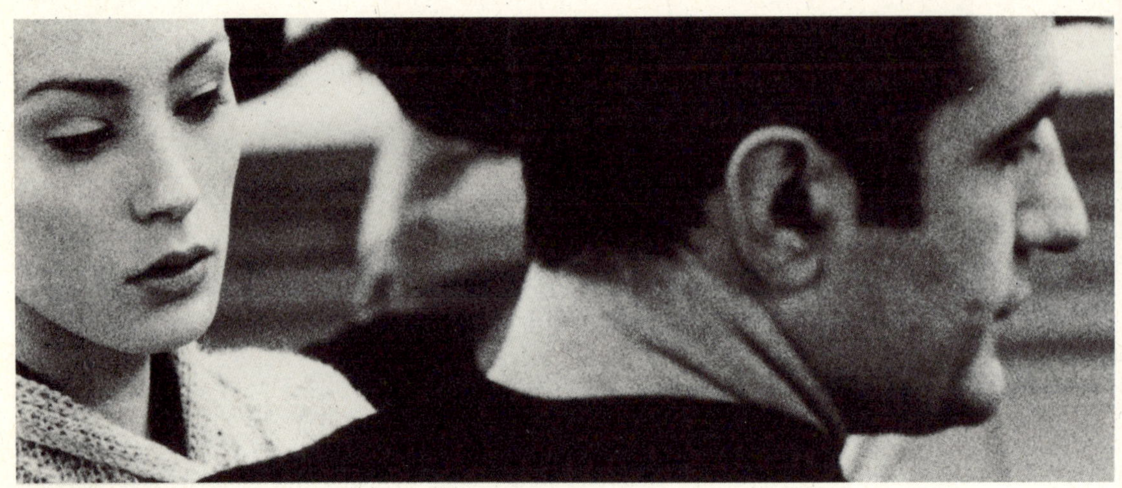

Scenarios, 1990's
b/w photo
104,7 x 209,6 cm
courtesy Galerie Gisela Capitain, Cologne

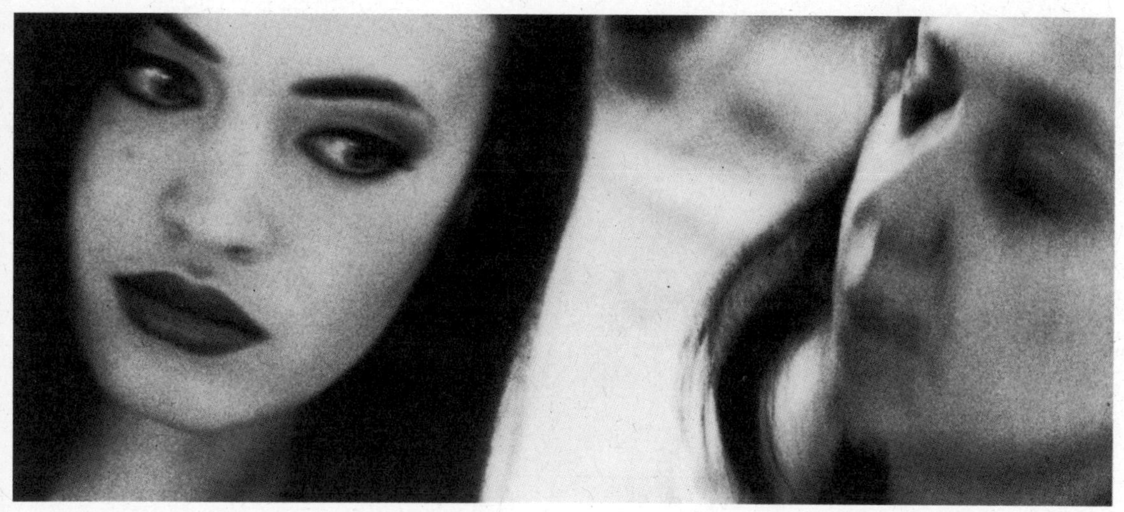

Allegories of Beauty (Incomplete), 1996
b/w photo
84,4 x 154,4 cm
courtesy Galerie Gisela Capitain, Cologne

Interview *by Adam Chodzko*

Adam Chodzko You have used interviews, haven't you, as part of your work?

Georgina Starr Yes, for *Getting to Know You*, I was asked twenty questions about the guy that I was trying to get to know. But they were all questions that I had constructed. I wanted to find out about a stranger, without ever meeting him. I chose this person from a big list of names because he had the same initials as me.

Chodzko And have you met him since?

Starr Our first meeting was very strange. I knew so much about him, really. Whatever he said couldn't really change the opinion that I already had of him. I had been sending him instructions such as to write up his dreams in the morning. I took these to a graphologist who told me how old he was, his birth sign, if he was married, how many children he had, what his personality was like; she said he was a writer and that his name was a pseudonym. It was all true, and she got all this from his handwriting. She said she was a little bit psychic as well. I also wanted to put myself through this investigation, so a friend took my handwriting to this woman and recorded the conversation with her.

All through the interview you can hear him saying "Oh my God! Oh my God", because everything she was saying was true.

Chodzko A lot of your other work was based on chance. The structure always evolved from a real scenario (*Whistling* and *Eric*) and often incorporated a group of strangers, but with the *Nine Collections of the Seventh Museum*, or *Visit to a Small Planet* the focus is on your own identity.

Starr That's true. It uses a mixture of other people and myself, but I am the subject.

Chodzko One of the doubts expressed in *Visit to a Small Planet* is that people do not speak their minds. Were you discovering this when you were investigating other people; that the results were so fictionalised because there wasn't any truth at the heart of it?

Starr With pieces such as *Getting to Know You* and *Visit to a Small Planet*, you can get a form of focus because they're actually based on real people. But I do *like* fiction; the fictional side of *Visit to a Small Planet* is just as important as my memory. My memory becomes a fiction because it is how I remember it. When I recently saw the film on which it is based it was completely different from *how* I remembered it. A memory is nothing until you backtrack and examine the context. It starts as a series of small incidents, and all of a sudden it becomes much richer and a whole new story erupts.

Chodzko So, instead of single truths you've been finding incredible fragmentation? When you are piecing together your own identity through a series of mementoes, memories and friends, there is always an infinite network of associations?

Starr But I really like all that. For instance, your opinion of friends changes every day. They might say something which makes you question why you liked them in the first place, or you might like them more. I think people modify their opinion the whole time.

Chodzko Although your work is constructing your history, as a viewer you don't have to have a prior knowledge of what your project is. With any piece you can start from scratch...

Starr Yes, otherwise you have to assume that people will understand what they are seeing only by referring to the catalogue essay. You are not then allowing people actually to begin and end a relationship with the work in front of them.

Chodzko A lot of recent work that develops a system or some kind of investigative procedure uses it to open up a space for the fantastic. We proceed through an activity that has its basis in quasi-scientific research, but use the process to catalyse the ridiculous and the extreme. In *Visit to a Small Planet,* there's desire for invisibility, aliens, mind-reading...

Starr That is what I really liked about doing *Visit to a Small Planet* — as you said before, does it reveal my identity or my disguise? I was *enjoying* it, even in a childish, playful way. What I like about this method of working is that you never know what's going to happen.

Chodzko But is this notion of play innocent? *Visit to a Small Planet* kept reminding me about a form of artistic space invasion with its mindreading aliens. Our artistic practice is an invasion of other people's space, which raises questions of morality. But turning attention more on to yourself in your work, do you now feel that kind of intrusion into your own space?

Starr The moral issue came up for some of us who were making work that involved people who would never fully know how they had become a part of an art work. A lot of the characters that I'm playing are based on people I know, my mother, a friend of mine, my sister. So, I'm still using other people in the work but I become a sort of vehicle for them.

It's also a question of setting up the viewer as voyeur; providing the capacity to look at someone's life in that much detail. *Crying* might appear to do that because it's more about sharing an intimacy than allowing for voyeurism. That's because the events and moments that I'm showing are so familiar to anybody. They're not that bizarre; they're things we all do. I've just highlighted them and given them a space where they can be contemplated.

Chodzko Yes, we're showing a private space in a public space, and there is a danger that it becomes pure spectacle with no relationship to the viewer's private space. It can be dismissed as passive entertainment with reactions such as "Oh, they're really weird, they enlarge chewing gum. I wouldn't do that."

Starr Exactly. But entertainment has to go into it, otherwise it's just 'interesting', I always make decisions about what it is that I would like to see. I hope the audience doesn't worry about my work but actually enjoys it, even participates in it. With *Visit to a Small Planet, Making Junior* and *The Party* I am also alleviating boredom by trying to entertain myself, so it makes sense that people looking at them should feel entertained.

Chodzko A lot of interesting art today has its visual aspect almost as a by-product of an activity.

Starr I *use* art because I'm not exactly sure what it is that I'm doing. If I weren't an artist but I was doing what I was doing, there'd be nowhere to put the products of the activity; I use the umbrella of art to give it a place. I always get a bit afraid that because I'm not specialising I could carry on for the rest of my life dealing with bits and pieces. On the other hand, we don't want to let a medium take over and restrict us.

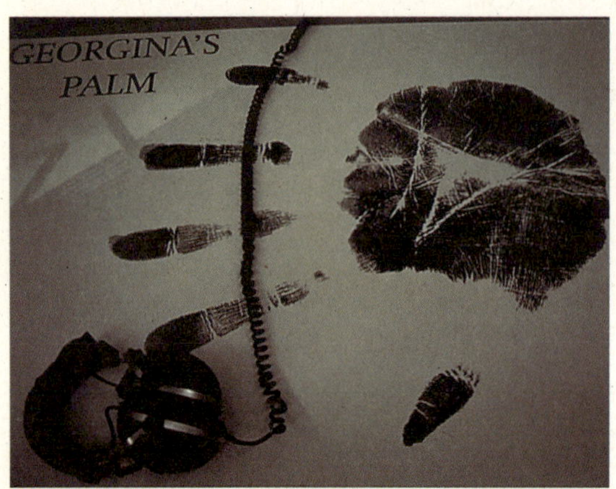

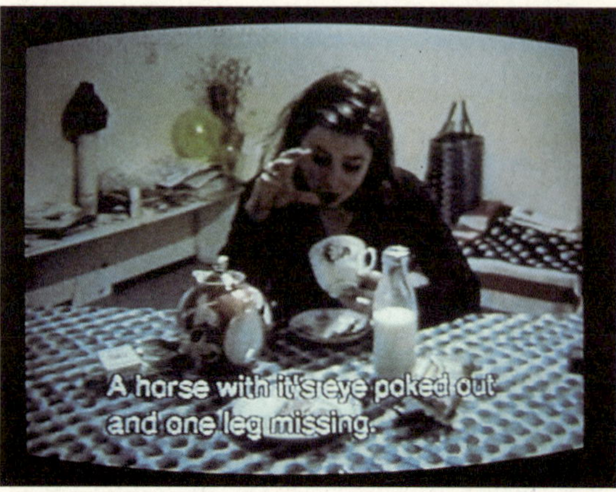

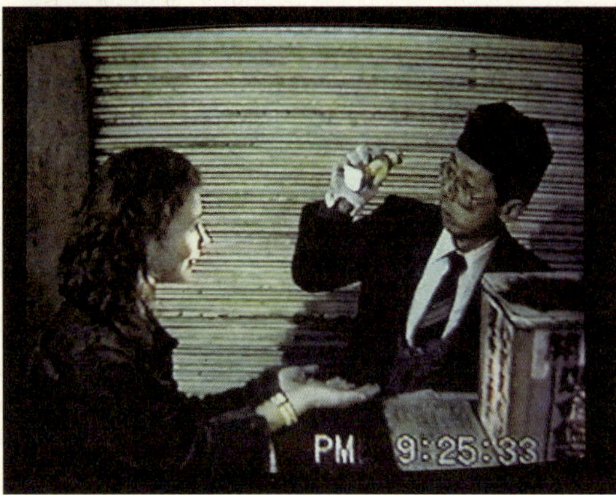

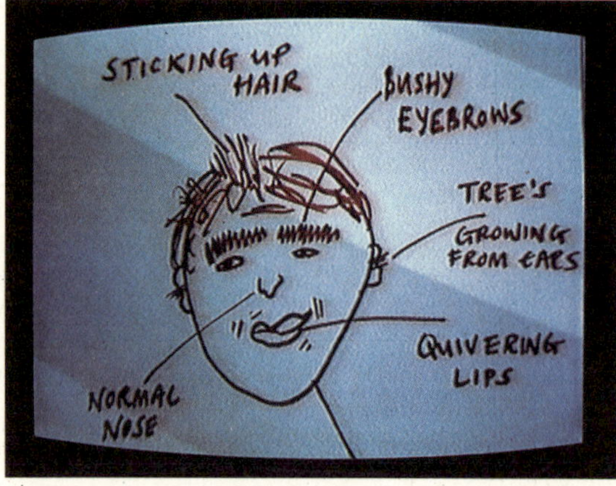

Getting to know You, 1993
installation, mixed media
courtesy the artist and Anthony Reynolds Gallery, London/Bloom Gallery, Amsterdam

PAGE 91-92
Oh! Daniel, 1996
colour lasers on aluminum
30 x 42 cm
courtesy the artist and Anthony Reynolds Gallery, London/Bloom Gallery, Amsterdam

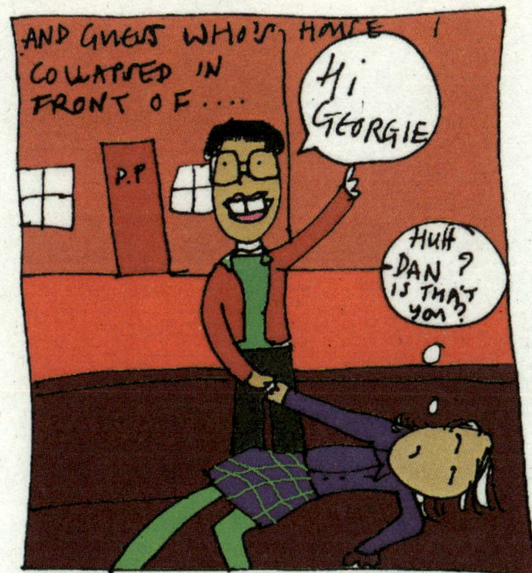
AND GUESS WHO'S HOUSE I COLLAPSED IN FRONT OF....
Hi GEORGIE
Huh? DAN? IS THAT YOU?
P.P

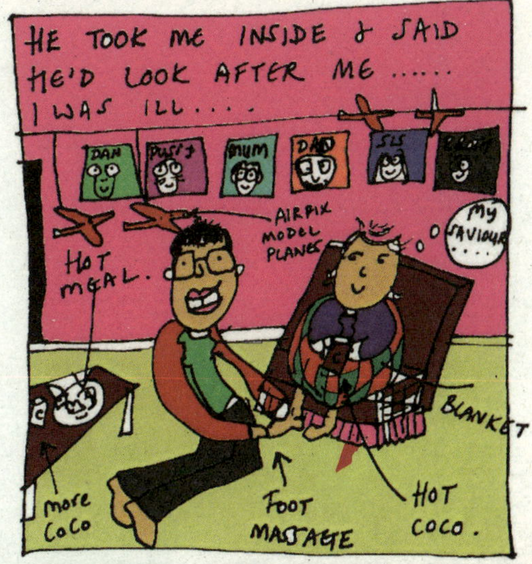
HE TOOK ME INSIDE & SAID HE'D LOOK AFTER ME ...... I WAS ILL....
DAN
PUSSY
MUM
DAD
SIS
AIRPIX MODEL PLANES
MY SAVIOUR
HOT MEAL.
BLANKET
MORE COCO
FOOT MASSAGE
HOT COCO.

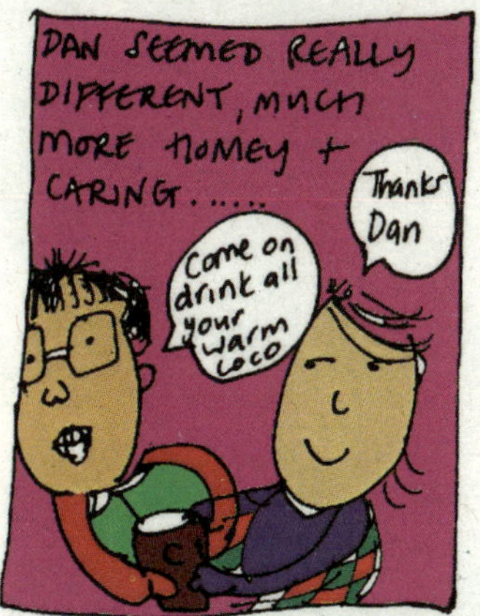
DAN SEEMED REALLY DIFFERENT, MUCH MORE HOMEY + CARING......
Thanks Dan
Come on drink all your warm COCO

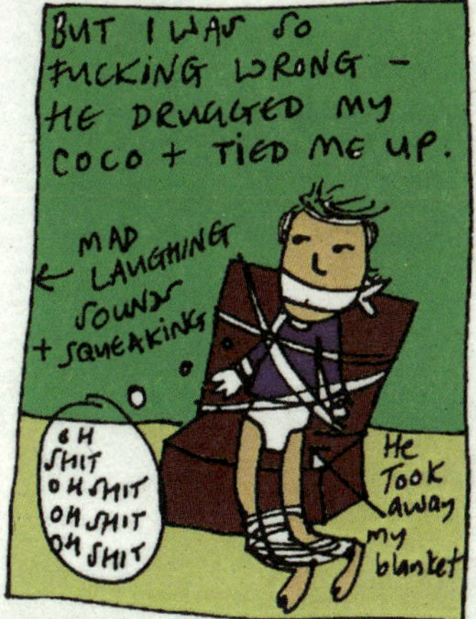
BUT I WAS SO FUCKING WRONG — HE DRUGGED MY COCO + TIED ME UP.
MAD LAUGHING SOUNDS + SQUEAKING
OH SHIT OH SHIT OH SHIT OH SHIT
He TOOK AWAY MY blanket

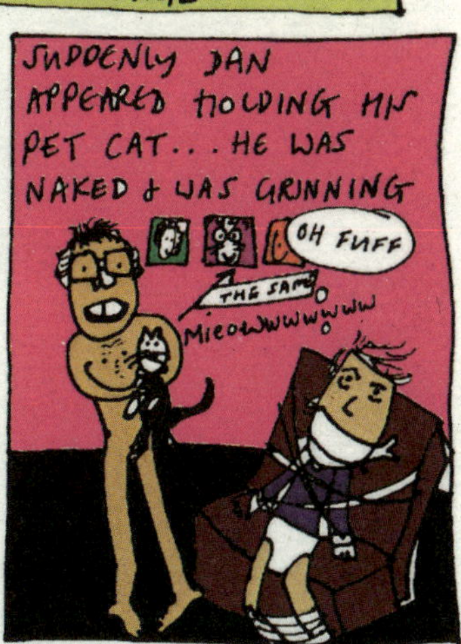
SUDDENLY DAN APPEARED HOLDING HIS PET CAT... HE WAS NAKED & WAS GRINNING
OH FUFF
THE SAME
MieoWWWWWWW

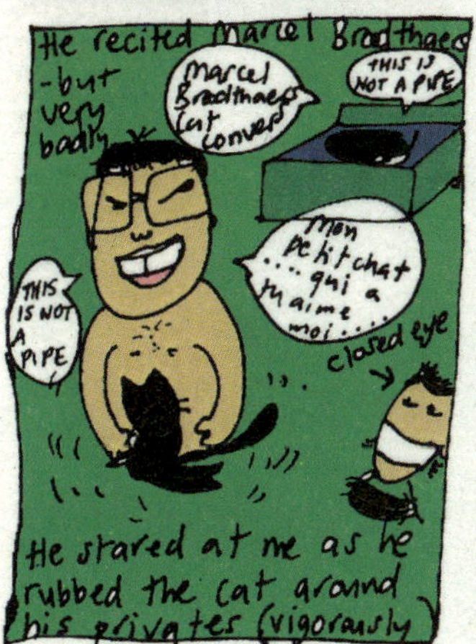
He recited Marcel Broodthaers —but very badly
Marcel Broodthaers Cat Convers
THIS IS NOT A PIPE
THIS IS NOT A PIPE
Mon petit chat qui m'aime moi
closed eye
He stared at me as he rubbed the cat around his privates (vigorously)

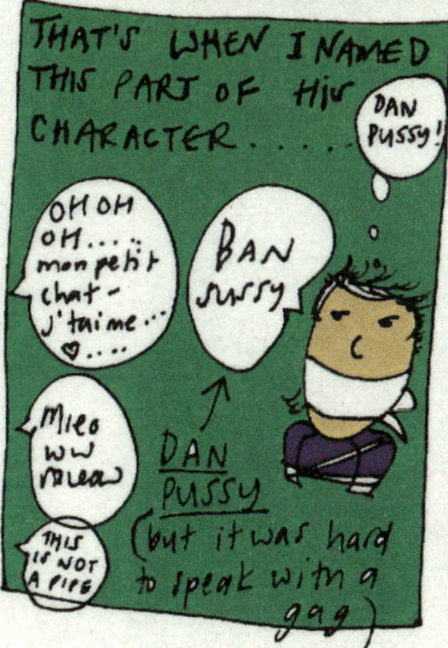
THAT'S WHEN I NAMED THIS PART OF HIS CHARACTER.....
DAN PUSSY!
OH OH OH.... mon petit chat - j'taime ... ♡ ....
DAN PUSSY
Mieo ww rolea
DAN PUSSY
THIS IS NOT A PIPE
(but it was hard to speak with a gag)

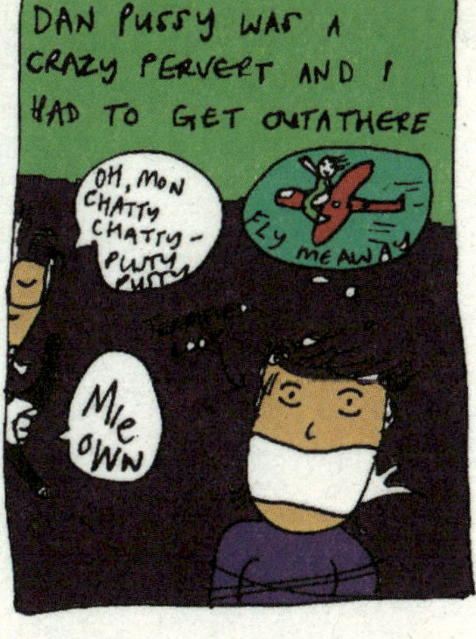
DAN PUSSY WAS A CRAZY PERVERT AND I HAD TO GET OUTATHERE
OH, MON CHATTY CHATTY - PUSSY PUSSY
FLY ME AWAY
Mie OWN

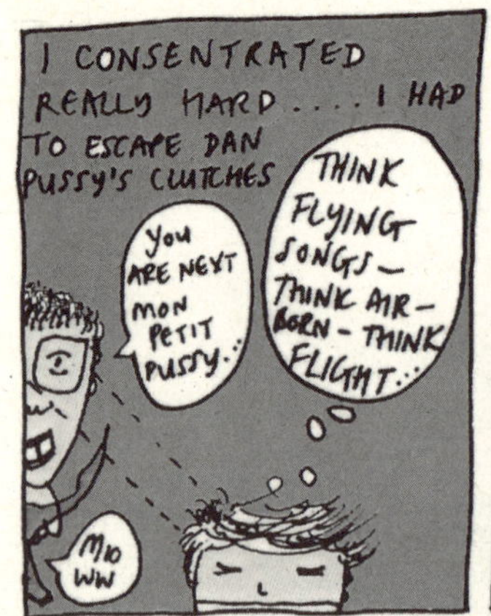

I CONSENTRATED REALLY HARD.... I HAD TO ESCAPE DAN PUSSY'S CLUTCHES
YOU ARE NEXT MON PETIT PUSSY...
THINK FLYING SONGS — THINK AIR-BORN — THINK FLIGHT...
MIO WW

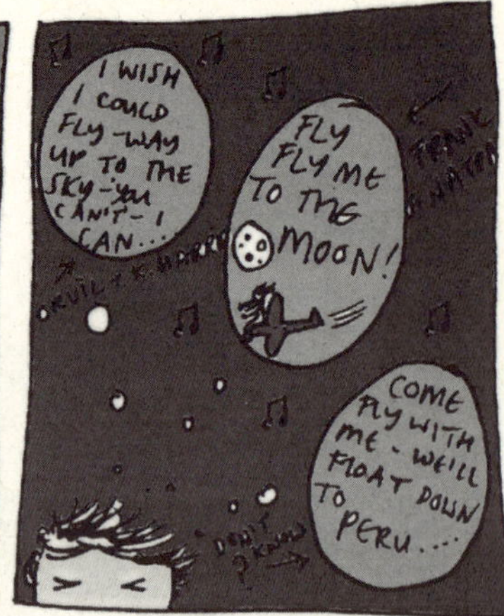

I WISH I COULD FLY-WAY UP TO THE SKY-YOU CAN'T-I CAN...
FLY FLY ME TO THE MOON!
COME FLY WITH ME - WE'LL FLOAT DOWN TO PERU....
DON'T KNOW

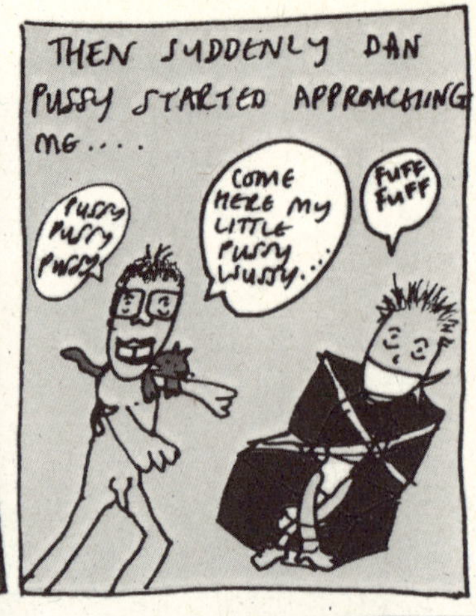

THEN SUDDENLY DAN PUSSY STARTED APPROACHING ME....
PUSSY PUSSY PUSSY
COME HERE MY LITTLE PUSSY WUSSY...
FUFF FUFF

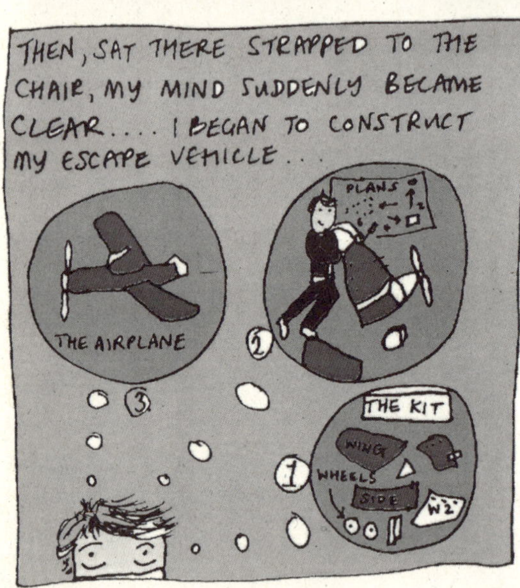

THEN, SAT THERE STRAPPED TO THE CHAIR, MY MIND SUDDENLY BECAME CLEAR.... I BEGAN TO CONSTRUCT MY ESCAPE VEHICLE...
THE AIRPLANE
PLANS
2
3
THE KIT
WING
WHEELS
SIDE
W2
1

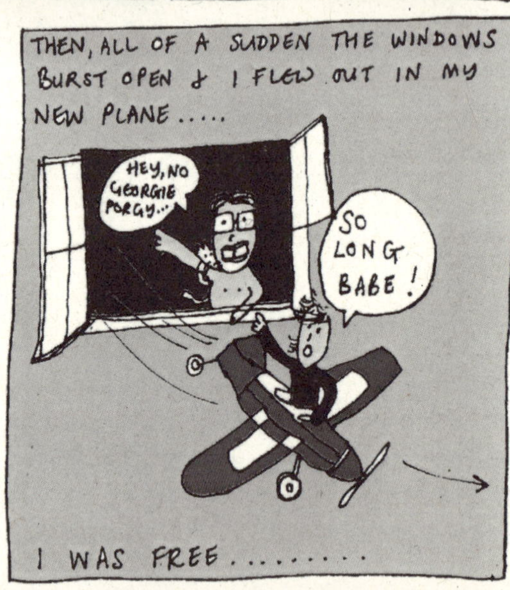

THEN, ALL OF A SUDDEN THE WINDOWS BURST OPEN & I FLEW OUT IN MY NEW PLANE.....
HEY, NO GEORGIE PORGY...
SO LONG BABE!
I WAS FREE.........

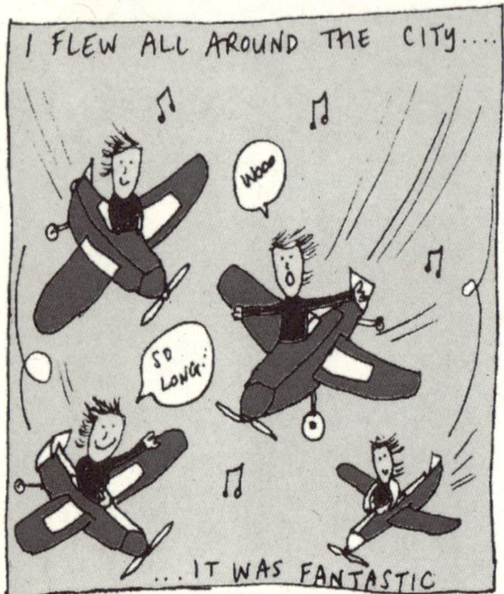

I FLEW ALL AROUND THE CITY....
WOOO
SO LONG...
...IT WAS FANTASTIC

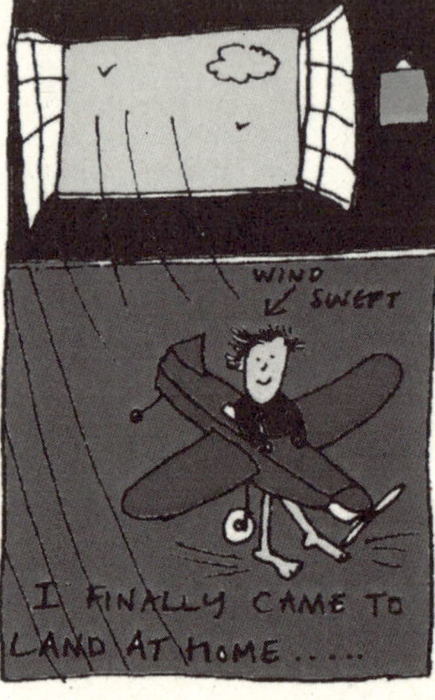

WIND SWEPT
I FINALLY CAME TO LAND AT HOME.....

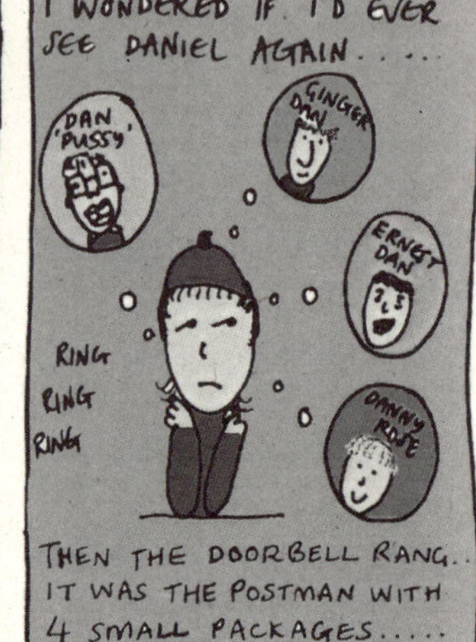

I WONDERED IF I'D EVER SEE DANIEL AGAIN.....
DAN 'PUSSY'
GINGER DAN
ERNST DAN
DANNY ROSE
RING RING RING
THEN THE DOORBELL RANG.. IT WAS THE POSTMAN WITH 4 SMALL PACKAGES.....

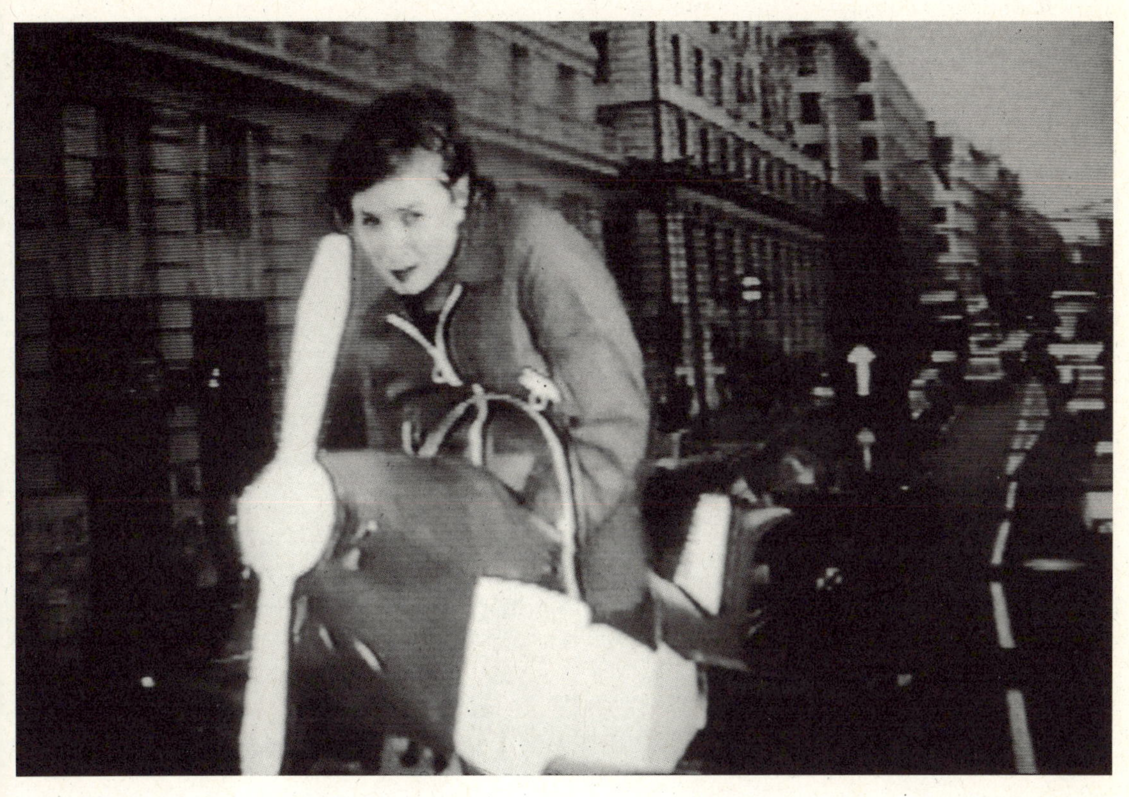

So long, Babe, 1996
video installation
courtesy the artist and Anthony Reynolds Gallery, London/Bloom Gallery, Amsterdam

Gillian Wearing

Say what you want

In 1991, Gillian Wearing took to the busy London streets and embarked on a series of photographs, descriptively entitled *Signs that say what you want them to say and not Signs that say what someone else wants you to say*. Confronted by the artist, members of the public were asked to write down on a sheet of paper exactly what was on their mind. The peculiarity of each statement, displayed by its author, compiles an absorbing account of day dreams, anxieties, personal beliefs and aspirations. One photograph shows an elderly woman holding out a sign which reads, 'I really love Regents Park', while an unshaven student opts for 'Everything is connected in life, the point is to know it and understand it'. Snapped throughout the early nineties, the series captured a nation in economic decline measured by signs such as 'Will England get through the recession' and another, gingerly disclosed by a smartly dressed company employee, which reads 'I'm desperate'. The images of London's homeless are particularly jarring. 'Give people homes, there is plenty of empty ones OK!'. The sign continues, 'I have been certified as mildly insane', and ends with a touching plea, 'Come back Mary, love you'. Glancing through Wearing's photographs, the compulsion is to marry each person's appearance with their sign, back and forth, until the image reveals itself as an attempt to enter the invisible realm of other people's mind. Where we would ordinary guess what people in the street are thinking, Wearing's signs endeavour to 'out' intangible thoughts and emotions.

In recent years, single screen videoworks and video installations superseded Wearing's photographic output which included the 'sign' series. Initially, the bridgework from one medium to another was imperceptible as Wearing continued to ask Londoners to perform a task within a predetermined framework. Yet again, a broad section of the general public forms the basis of *Confess all on Video. Don't worry you'll be in Disguise. Intrigued? Call Gillian ...* (1994). The wording of the title refers to an advert placed in *Time Out Magazine* which invited people to come forward and confess their innermost secrets. As promised, those who took up the offer are heavily disguised in a variety of wigs and masks, which number amongst them Ronald Reagan and Neil Kinnock. One after the other, a man confesses to sleeping with a prostitute, another to being gay and making obscene phone calls, and a woman who, after she discovered her boyfriend was having an affair, drugged him, stole his credit cards and left him naked in a hotel room. An intriguing confession comes from a man unable to forget — his own words are 'file away' — the experience in his youth of watching his brother 'snog' his two sisters. As with the 'Sign' series, Wearing's adherence to a preconceived framework ensures that the early videoworks are as unpredictable as the people they contain. More recently, however, Wearing's line of enquiry has focused on a more concise portrayal of the characters she encounters in everyday life.

In 1994, Wearing filmed herself dancing in a South London shopping mall. Aptly entitled *Dancing in Peckham*, she throws herself into an energetic dance routine without any musical accompaniment. Passers-by look on in bewilderment, clearly perplexed and unaware that, prior to her performance, Wearing memorised Nirvana's 'Smells Like Teen Spirit' and Gloria Gaynor's 'I Will Survive'. Played out in her mind, Wearing moves to a rhythm which only she can hear. *Homage to the Woman with the bandaged Face who I saw Yesterday down the Walworth Road* (1995) refers to a busy South London high street. Disguised behind a mask of bandages, Wearing's facial garb in *Homage ...* is inspired by two people who left a lasting impression on the artist. The first, a girl believed to be on her way to a night-club in London's West End, the second, an Afro-Caribbean woman — often seen in the Walworth Road — who persistently paints her face white due to a rare form of psychological affliction. Further evidence of Wearing's streetwise inspiration occurs in *Western Security* (1995); a video and sound installation exhibited at London's Hayward Gallery that features a mock shoot-out between a bunch of rampaging cowboys. *Western Security* is largely inspired by her observation of men whose past-time it is to dress up as Clint Eastwood and parade about the streets of South London.

Wearing's video triptych *The Unholy Three* (1996) constitutes a fly on the wall glimpse at the private lives of a real life South London cowboy nick-named Young Guns, an acute caffeine addict who literally drinks tea in buckets, and glamour

girl Claire who performs a series of risqué manoeuvres with an inflatable
champagne bottle. All three eventually meet on a blind date in a pub where the
two men find themselves at loggerheads over Claire who is not in the least bit
interested in either of them. Wearing's most recent installation *60 Minutes Silence*
(1996) is a cinematic-scale video back projection of members of the police force
posing for what appears to be a year book photograph. Asked to stay absolutely
still for over an hour — as though they were undergoing some form of endurance-
test — the police become increasingly uncomfortable with each passing minute.
Ultimately, the video places people who are perceived as having control over us, in
a controlled situation.

Seemingly, when asked, people will do anything for Wearing, whether it be
confess all, or say what they want with signs. However, both *The Unholy Three*
and *60 Minutes Silence*, represent a subtle departure as Wearing continues to
choreograph members of the public, only this time within the confines of a
loosely scripted film. While the parameters of the early work were set by pen and
paper, camera and confession, the present framework — into which people are
placed and asked to perform — suggests a shift from understated to direct
intervention. The space to watch, so to speak, is the journey from what other
people might want to say, to how Wearing instructs them to perform.

Gregor Muir

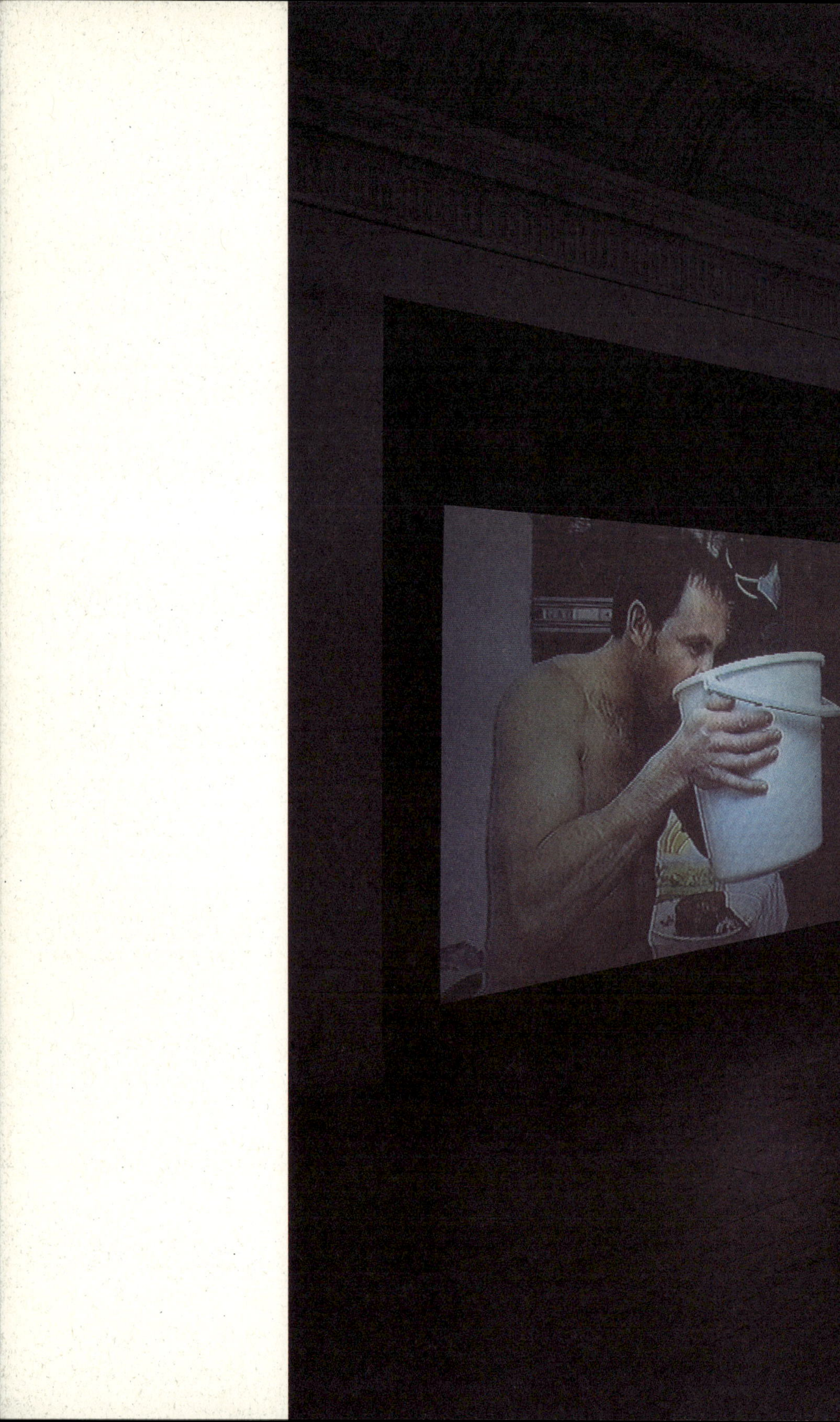

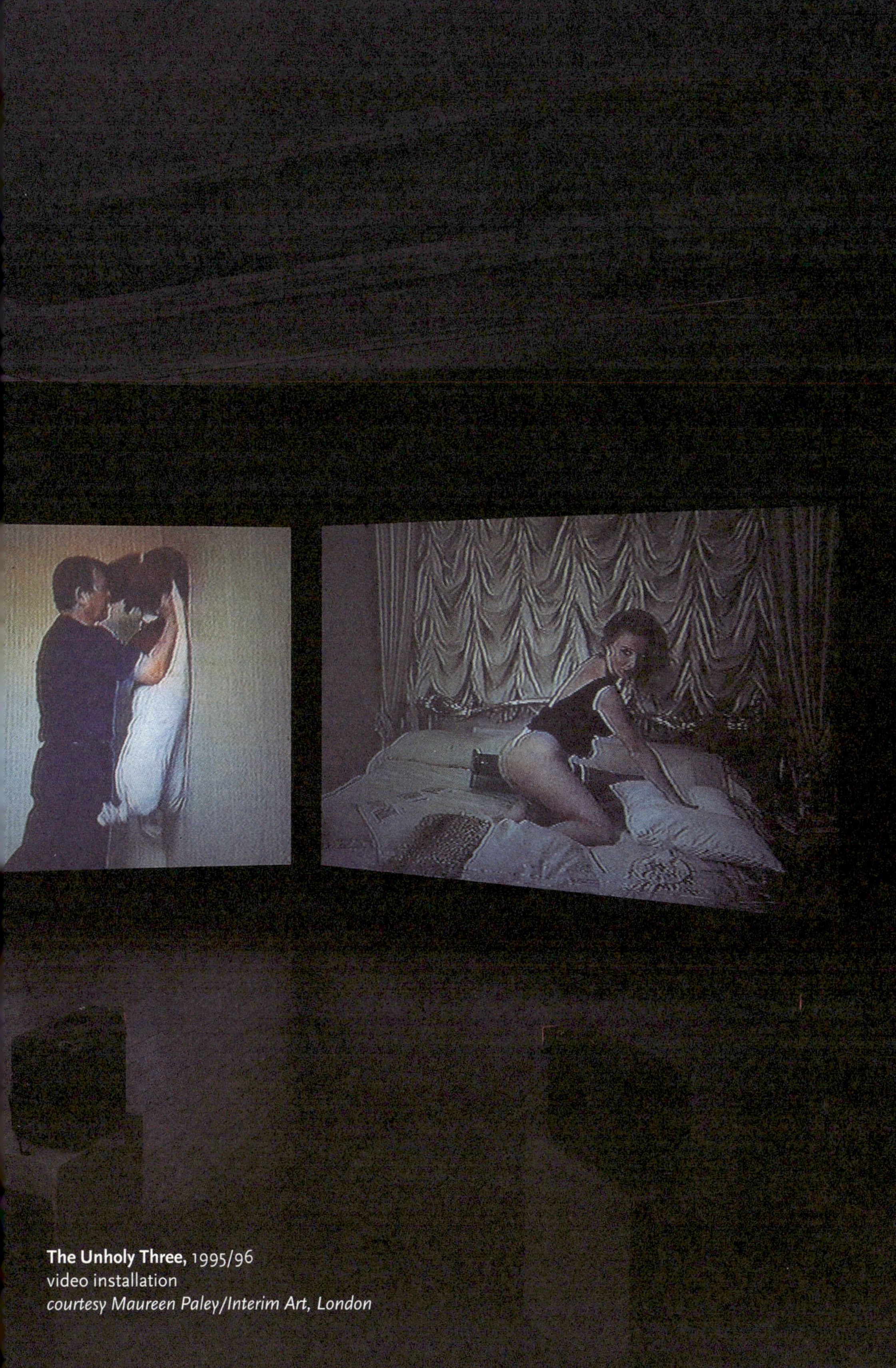

The Unholy Three, 1995/96
video installation
courtesy Maureen Paley/Interim Art, London

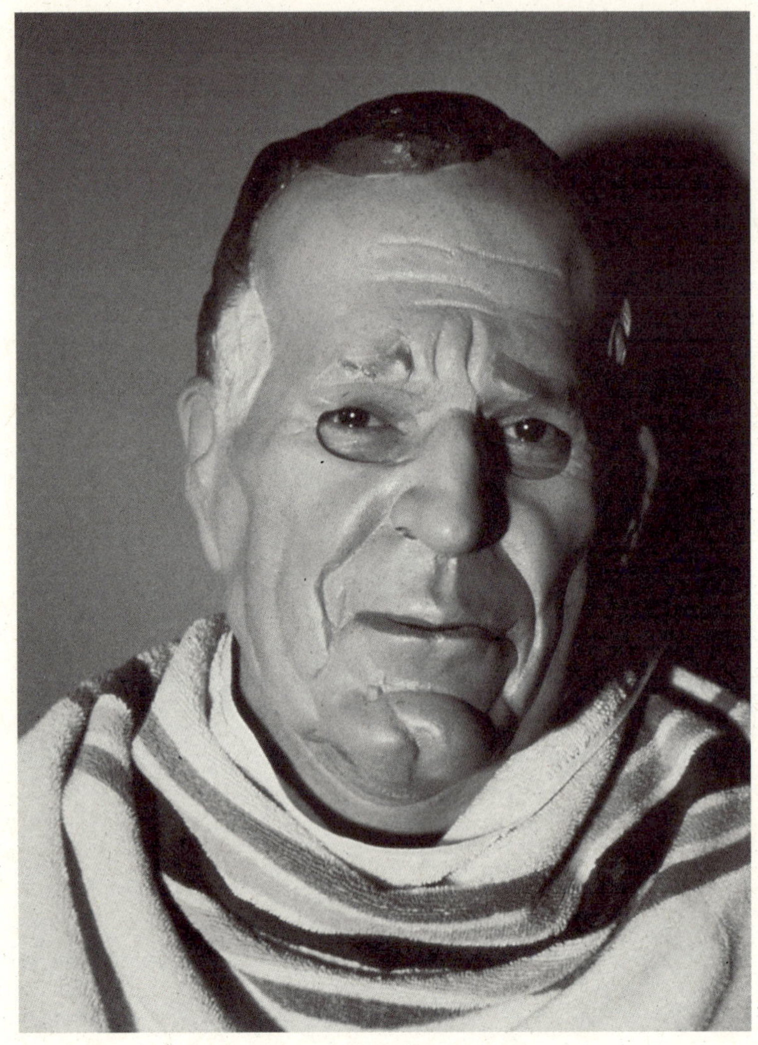

Confess all on Video. Don't Worry you'll be in Disguise. Intrigued? Call Gillian..., 1994
video
courtesy Maureen Paley/Interim Art, London

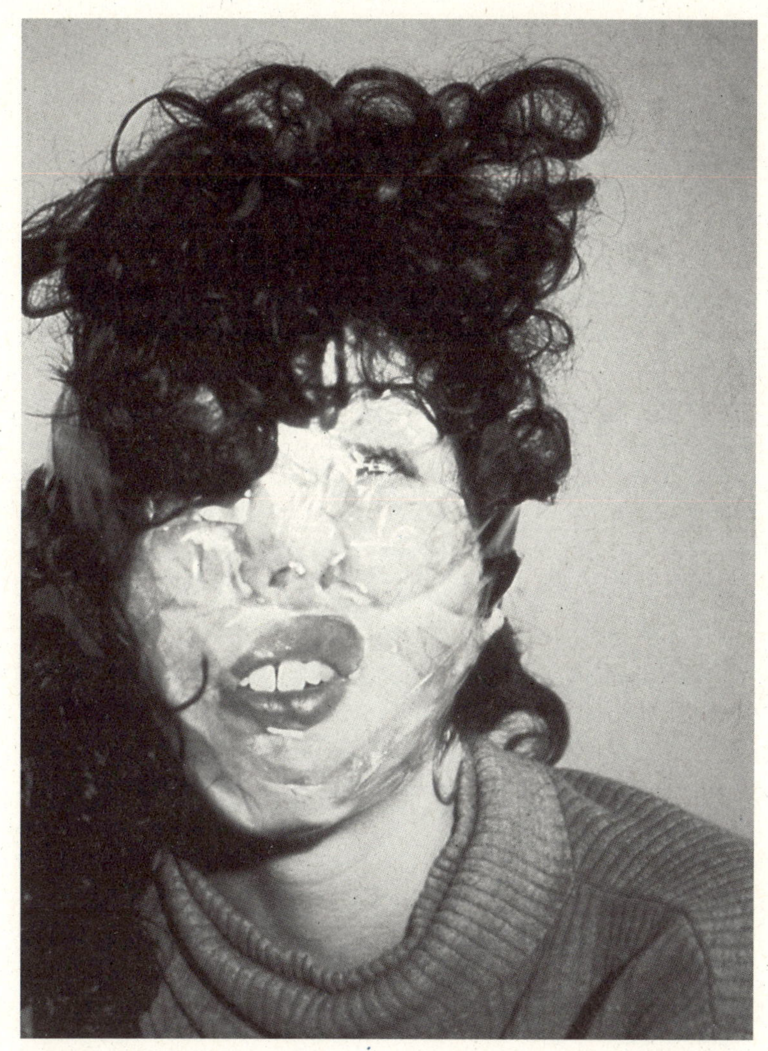

Eija-Liisa Ahtila

1959
Born in Finland
Lives and works in Helsinki

1980-1985
Helsinki University, Helsinki
1990-1991
London College of Printing, School of Media and
Management, Film and Video Department, London
1994-1995
UCLA, Certificate Program, Film, TV, Theatre and
Multimedia Studies, Los Angeles
1994-1995
American Film Institute, Advanced Technology
Program special courses, Los Angeles

Awards and grants

1988,1989,1992
Finnish Cultural Foundation
1989, 1991, 1994
Center of Audiovisual Promotion
1990
Young Artist of the Year
Paulo Foundation
1991, 1993, 1995
Visek: The foundation for the support of
audiovisual art
1992
The Central Committee for the Arts, a 3-year
grant
1995
The Central Committee for the Arts, a 1-year grant

Essays for *Taide-Finnish Art Magazine*, since 1987
Essays and visual supplements for *Siksi-Nordic
Art Review*

Film-Video

1988
The Nature of Things
(12min.; VHS, written & directed by
E.L. Ahtila & Maria Ruotsala)
Screenings (a selection):
Audiovisual Biennale of Video, Arnhem
Tampere International Film Festival, Finland
1991
Plato's Son

(35 min.; Betacam SP; written & directed by
E.L. Ahtila & Maria Ruotsala)
1993
The Trial
(17 min.; 1993; Betacam SP; written & directed by
E.L. Ahtila & V.M. Saarinen, directed by E.L. Ahtila)
Screenings:
The Kitchen, New York
YLE TV-1, Finland
Me/We, Okay, Gray: A production of three 90
seconds audio visual stories/films which are
presented both as independent works, amongst
trailers in cinemas and on televison channels,
shown between advertisements and programs.
(S-16/35mm; written & directed by E.L. Ahtila)
Screenings (a selection):
TV YLE TV-1, Finland
ARTE, G.E.I.E., Germany & France
Kunstkanaal, Holland
SBS-channel, Australia
Festivals (a selection):
Oberhausen International Film Festival,
Oberhausen
Melbourne International Film Festival,
Melbourne
São Paulo International Film Festival, São Paulo
Other screenings:
Director's Guild of America, Los Angeles
'Reading Room', Project Camden Arts Center,
London
'Fordomar', Lilljevalchs Art Hall, Stockholm
'Identity', Helsinki and Moscow
1995
If 6 was 9, A film and video installation
(16/35mm; written & directed by E.L. Ahtila)
Galleri Index, Stockholm, Sweden and touring in
Scandinavia
Screenings (a selection):
Kino Engel, Helsinki
1996
'NowHere',Lousiana Museum of Modern Art,
Humlebaek

Installations

1989
In His Absolute Proximity, Photo-text (poems)
installation
Gallery Katariina, Helsinki
Museum of Contemporary Art, Helsinki
1990
Teacher, Teacher!, Photos, texts-poems, objects

The Young Artist of the Year, Tampere Art
Museum, Tampere
Wonderland, Photo-text installation
Scandinavian Art Biennale, Reykjavik & Helsinki
1991
The Tender Trap, Slides projected on wooden
elements, a script-text, a soundtrack
'Seeing', The opening exhibition of the Museum
of Contemporary Art, Helsinki
Kluuvi Gallery, Helsinki
1993
Dog Bites, Photo installation
Lilljevalchs Art Hall, Stockholm
1994
Secret Garden, Multimedia installation
Hameenlinna Art Museum, Finland
1996
Through, Moving image installation in three
monitors
Beaconfield Gallery, London
If 6 Was 9, Moving image installation
Lousiana Museum of Modern Art, Humlebaek
Galleri Index, Stockholm
Gable Gallery, Helsinki
Station 96, Gothenburg

Performances (a selection)

1988
A Short Cultural-Political Quadrille,
Small Theatre, Lahti Audiovisual Biennale, Finland
1989
Jokes, Performed at the 125 Year Jubilee of the
Artist Association in Finland

Vanessa Beecroft

1969
Born in Genova
Lives and works in New York

Solo exhibitions (a selection)

1994
Schipper & Krome, Cologne
Fac-Simile, Milan
1995
Galerie Analix, Geneva
1996
Galerie Ghislaine Hussenot, Paris
Galleria Massimo De Carlo, Milan
Galerie Tre, Stockholm
Galerie Analix, Geneva
Jeffrey Deitch Projects, New York

Group exhibitions (a selection)

1994
'Incertaine Identité', Galerie Analix, Geneva
'Winter of Love', P.S.1, New York
'Soggetto-Soggetto', Castello di Rivoli, Torino
(cat.)
'Prima Linea', Trevi Flash Art Museum, Trevi (cat.)
1995
'Show Must Go On', Fondation Cartier pour l'Art
Contemporain, Paris
'This Is Today' (trailer), Mediapark, Cologne
'Videos et Films d'Artistes', Atelier d'Artistes,
Marseilles
'Campo '95', Corderie dell'Arsenale, Castello,
Venice (cat.)
'Aperto Italia '95', Trevi Flash Art Museum, Trevi
(cat.)
'Fuori Uso '95', Ex Aurum, Pescara (cat.)
'Anni 90 Arte a Milano', Palazzo delle Stelline,
Milan (cat.)
1996
'Moving', Projektraum, Zurich
'A/Drift: Scenes from the Penetrable Culture',
Center for Cultural Studies, Bard College, New
York (cat.)
'Ultime Generazioni: Esposizione Nazionale
Quadriennale d'Arte di Roma', Q XII, Rome
'Shopping', Jeffrey Deitch Projects, New York
(cat.)
'Fri-Art', Centre d'Art Contemporain Kunsthalle,

Fribourg
'Persona', Kunsthalle, Basel
'Push-Ups', The Factory, Athens Fine Arts School,
Athens
'Conversation Pieces II', Institute of
Contemporary Art, Philadelphia (cat.)
'Persona', The Renaissance Society, Chicago
'Aufnahmen der Normalität', Galerie der Stadt
Schwaz, Vienna
'Everything That's Interesting Is New', The Dakis
Joannou Collection, Athens (cat.)
'Traffic', CAPC Musée d'Art Contemporain,
Bordeaux (cat.)

Performances

1994
Andrea Rosen Gallery, New York
'Mädchen in Uniform', Galleria Massimo De
Carlo, Milan
VHS, Giacinto Di Pietrantonio, Milan
1995
'Analix: Art'26 1995', Kunstmesse, Basel
1996
'Museumfest', Wallraf-Richartz-Museum &
Museum Ludwig, Cologne
'Everything That's Interesting Is New', The
Factory, Athens Fine Arts School, Athens

Articles and reviews (a selection)

1993
P. Groot, *Het krijtwitte kind*, Amsterdam
1994
M.A. Korovkin, 'Invirtù della realtà: Mass-media e
violenza', *Juliet*, No.70
'Incertaine Identité', Galerie Analix, Geneva
H. Papadopoulos, 'Vanessa Beecroft', *Bob*, No.1
G. Di Pietrantonio, 'Vanessa Beecroft: Ouverture',
Flash Art, Vol.28, No.183, Summer, pp.118-119
'V. Beecroft, Purple Bustes', *Purple Prose*, No.6
G. Di Pietrantonio, 'Film: Review', *ARTI*, No.17
1995
E. Favereau, 'Vous', *Liberation*, Dec 1
'AAVV', XXI *Arte e Architettura*
B. Polla, 'Vanessa Beecroft: Review', *Documents*,
No.7
'Ein blonder Traum: Performance', *ZAPP-
magazine*, No.4
E. Janus, 'Vanessa Beecroft: Opening', *Artforum
International*, No.9, May, pp.92-93
B. Polla, 'Les filles sont inconscientes de la
portée de leur image', *Purple Prose*, No.8
J. Roberts, 'Vanessa Beecroft: Review', *Frieze*,
No.20
W. Furlong, 'Interview', *Audio Arts Magazine*,
Vol.14, No.3
L. Cherubini, 'Vanessa Beecroft: Strange Girls',
El Guia, No.4
F. Pasini, 'Finale di Partita', Castelvetro
1996
Purple Fashion, No.2
L. Gugliemi, *La Republica*, Oct 1
C. Colasanti, 'Trend Arts', *Trend*, No.9, Sept
B. Steiner, 'Film as a Method of Thinking and
Working', *Paletten*, Vol.1, No.224
A. Bulloch, 'On a Vanessa Beecroft Performance',
The Guardian, July 9
A. Smith, 'Art & Leisure', *The New York Times*,
May
A. Vettese, 'Art in Milan', *Parkett*, No.46, Summer
L. Marucci, 'Vanessa Beecroft: Interview', *Juliet*,
No.78, June
M.V.Carloni, 'La Mia Moda e' come una
Performance', *Panorama*, No.23, June
G. Romano, 'Todo lo que es interessante es
nuevo', *Lapiz*, No.122, June
C. Christov-Bakargiev, 'Vanessa e le sue sorelle',
L'Espresso, No.18, May
'Visioni del nuovo mondo', *Max*, No.5, May
'Everything That's Interesting Is New', *Flash Art*,
Vol.28, No.197, May
M. Casadio, 'Pelle d'artista', *Vogue*, No.548, April
'AAVV Colezionismo a Torino', *Charta*

Willie Doherty

1959
Born in Derry, Northern Ireland
Lives and works in Derry

1978-1981
Ulster Polytechnic, Belfast

Awards

1995
'Glen Dimplex Artists Awards', Irish Museum of
Modern Art, Dublin

Solo exhibitions (a selection)

1986
'Photoworks', Oliver Dowling Gallery, Dublin
'Stone Upon Stone', Redemption!, Derry
1987
'The Town of Derry', Photoworks, Art & Research
Exchange, Belfast
1988
'Two Photoworks', Third Eye Center, Glasgow
'Colourworks', Oliver Dowling Gallery, Dublin
1990
'Imagined Truths', Oliver Dowling Gallery, Dublin
'Same Difference', Matt's Gallery, London
'Unknown Depths', John Hansard Gallery,
Southampton; Angel Row Gallery, Nottingham;
ICA Institute of Contemporary Arts, London;
Ffotogallery, Cardiff; Third Eye Center, Glasgow;
Orchard Gallery, Derry (cat.)
1991
Galerie Giovanna Minelli, Paris
'Kunst Europa, Six Irishman', Kunstverein
Schwetzingen, Schwetzingen
Tom Cugliani Gallery, New York
Oliver Dowling Gallery, Dublin
1992
Tom Gugliani Gallery, New York
Oliver Dowling Gallery, Dublin
Peter Kilchmann Gallery, Zurich
1993
'They're All the Same', Centre for Contemporary
Art, Ujazdoski Castel, Warsaw
'30 January 1972', Douglas Hyde Gallery, Dublin
'The Only Good One is a Dead One', Arnolfini,
Bristol; Matt's Gallery, London; Grey Art Gallery,
New York (cat.)

Galerie Jennifer Flay, Paris
1994
'At the End of the Day', British School at Rome,
Rome (brochure)
1995
Galerie Jennifer Flay, Paris
Peter Kilchmann Gallery, Zurich
Kerlin Gallery, Dublin
1996
Alexander and Bonin, New York
'The Only Good One is a Dead One', Edmonton
Art Gallery, Edmonton, Alberta (cat.)
'The Only Good One is a Dead One', Mendel Art
Gallery, Saskatchewan
'The Only Good One is a Dead One', Fondação
Calouste Gulbenkian, Centro de Arte Moderna,
Lisbon
Galleria Emi Fontana, Milan
ARC Musée d'Art Moderne de la Ville de Paris,
Paris
'No Smoke without Fire', Matt's Gallery, London
(cat.)
'In the dark. Projected works; Im Dunkeln.
Projizierte Arbeiten', Kunsthalle Bern, Bern (cat.)

Group exhibitions (a selection)

1987
'Directions Out', Douglas Hyde Gallery, Dublin
'The State of the Nation', Herbert Art Gallery,
Coventry
'A Line of Country', Cornerhouse, Manchester
'Ireland/Germany Exchange', Guiness Hop
Store, Dublin; Ulster Museum, Belfast
1988
'Three artists', Battersee Arts Centre, London
'Metro Billboard Project', Projects UK-Billboard
shown in Newcastle, Leeds, Manchester, Derry
and London
'Art for the Dart', A project on Dublin's suburban
rail link, organized by the Douglas Hyde Gallery,
Dublin
'Matter of Facts', Musée des Beaux Arts, Nantes;
Musée d'Art Moderne, St. Etienne; Metz pour la
Photographie, Metz (cat.)
1989
'Three artists', London Street, Derry
'Through the Looking Glass', Barbican Art
Gallery, London (cat.)
'I', Internationale Foto Triennale, Esslingen
(cat.)

1990

'False Dawn', Billboard project organized by Irish Exhibition of Living Art, Dublin

'Billboard Project', Irish Exhibition of Living Art, Dublin

'The British Art Show', South Bank Centre, London; McLellan Galleries, Glasgow; Leeds City Art Gallery, Leeds; Hayward Gallery, London (cat.)

'A New Tradition', Douglas Hyde Gallery, Dublin (cat.)

1991

'Denonciation', La Difference/GNAC, Usine Fromage, Darnetal; Centre d'Art Santa Monica, Barcelona (cat.)

'Shocks to the System', South Bank Centre, London; Royal Festival Hall, London; Ikon Gallery, Birmingham (cat.)

'Europe Unknown', WKS Wawel, Ministry of Culture, Krakow (cat.)

'A place for art?', The Showroom, London

'Kunst Europa', AdKV, Germany (cat.)

'Inheritance and Transformation', The Irish Museum of Modern Art, Dublin (cat.)

'Outer Skin', South Bank Centre, London (cat.)

'Camera Austria 37 Symposium Exhibition', Graz (cat.)

1992

'Political Landscapes: Perspektief 43', Perspektief, Rotterdam (cat.)

'13 Critics 26 Photographers', Centre d'Art Santa Monica, Barcelona (cat.)

'Moltiplici Culture', Convento di S.Egidio, Rome (cat.)

'A Nation Once Again', Street poster commisioned by Transmission Gallery, Glasgow as part of 'Outta Here'

'It's Written All Over My Face', Billboard poster commissioned by the BBC Billboard Project as part of the Commissions and Collaborations Season

'Beyond Glory: Representing Terrorism', College of Art Maryland Institute, Baltimore

1993

'An Irish Presence', Venice Biennale, Venice

'Critical Landscapes', Tokyo Metropolitan Museum of Photography, Tokyo (cat.)

'Prospect 93', Frankfurter Kunstverein, Frankfurt (cat.)

'Krieg', Neue Galerie, Graz (cat.)

1994

'Cocido y Crudo', Museo Nacional Centro de Reina Sofia, Madrid (cat.)

'Willie Doherty, Peter Doig, Antony Gormley, Shirazeh Houshiary: The Turner Prize 1994', Tate Gallery, London

'Willie Doherty, Mona Hatoum, Doris Salcedo', Brooke Alexander, New York

'Point of interest, Points of Departure, John Berggruen Gallery, San Francisco

'From Beyond the Pale: Selected Works and Projects, part 1', Irish Museum of Modern Art, Dublin

'Installation', Washington Square Windows, Grey Art Gallery, New York

'Kraji Places', Moderna Galerija Ljubljana, Museum of Modern Art, Slovenia (cat.)

'The Spine', Foundation De Appel, Amsterdam (cat.)

'The Act of Seeing (Urban Space)', Foundation pour l'Architecture, Brussels

1995

'IMMA/Glen Dimplex Artists Awards', The Irish Museum of Modern Art, Dublin (cat.)

'Willie Doherty, Andreas Gursky', Moderna Museet, Stockholm

'Trust', Tramway, Glasgow

'It's Not a Picture', Galleria Emi Fontana, Milan

'New Art in Britain', Muzeum Sztuki, Lodz (cat.)

'Double Play-Beyond Cognition', Sint-Niklaas Stadsacademie, Sint-Niklaas

'Sites of Being', ICA Institute of Contemporary Art, Boston

'Distant Relations', Ikon Gallery, Birmingham; Camden Arts Centre, London; Irish Museum of Modern Art, Dublin

1996

'Happy End', Kunsthalle Düsseldorf, Dusseldorf

The 10th Biennale of Sydney, Sydney (cat.)

'Devant l'Histoire', Centre Georges Pompidou, Paris

Public Projects

1995

'Make Believe', A poster project for British Rail Mainline Stations

'The Space Between', Video installation, El Puento de Vizcaya, Bilbao

Articles and reviews (a selection)

1991

D. Drier, 'Same Difference', A project by Willie Doherty for *Artforum*, Vol.29, No.9, May, p.121

'They're All the Same', A project for *Frieze*, No.2

1993

R. Jennings, 'Willie Doherty: Matt's Gallery', *Time Out*, Dec

I. Blazwick, 'Interview with Willie Doherty', *Art Monthly*, No. 172, Dec-Jan, pp.3-7

1994

D. Cameron, 'Social Studies' *Art & Auction*, Nov

R. Cork, 'Muting the howls of the Philistines', *The Times* July 23

J. Kastner, 'Willie Doherty: Matt's Gallery', *Frieze*, No.14, Jan-Febr, pp.50-51

S. Morgan, 'The Spine: De Appel, Amsterdam', *Frieze*, No.16, May, p.52-53

A. Renton, 'Willie Doherty: Matt's Gallery', *Flash Art*, Vol.27, No.174, Jan-Feb, p.104

I. Schaffner, 'Willie Doherty: Grey Art Gallery', *Artforum*, Vol.33, No.4, Dec, p.85

R. Smith, 'Willie Doherty, Mona Hatoum and Doris Salcedo', *The New York Times*, Nov 11

R. Smith, 'Bluntly, the tragedy of 'the Troubles'', *The New York Times*, Sept 9

1995

J. Kastner, 'Ten Artists to Watch Worldwide: Willie Doherty, Northern Ireland', *ARTnews*, Jan, p.40

T. Maul, 'Willie Doherty', *Journal of Contemporary Art*, Vol.7, No.2, pp. 18-27

P. Rowlands, 'Willie Doherty: Jennifer Flay' *ARTnews*, Summer, p.135

1996

J. Higgins, 'Report from Ireland-Art at the Edge (Part II)', *Art in America*, Apr

G. Volk, 'Willie Doherty-Alexander and Bonin' *ARTnews*, Apr

J. Fish, 'Willie Doherty', in cat. *Willie Doherty: The Only Good One is a Dead One*, The Edmonton Art Gallery, Edmonton, Alberta

Douglas Gordon

1966
Born in Glasgow
Lives and works in Glasgow

1984-1988
Glasgow School of Art, Glasgow
1988-1990
Slade School of Art, London

Awards

1996
The Turner Prize, London

Solo exhibitions (a selection)

1993
'24 Hour Psycho', Tramway, Glasgow; Kunstwerke, Berlin (cat.)
'Migrateur', ARC Musée d'Art Moderne de la Ville de Paris, Paris (cat.)
1994
Lisson Gallery, London
'Bad Faith', Künstlerhaus Stuttgart, Stuttgart
1995
'The End', Jack Tilton Gallery, New York
'Jukebox', The Agency, London
'Entr'Acte 3', Stedelijk Van Abbemuseum, Eindhoven (cat.)
'24 Hour Psycho', Centre Georges Pompidou, Paris
Rooseum, Malmö
1996
'Douglas Gordon & Rirkrit Tiravanija', FRAC Languedoc-Roussillon, Montpellier
'24 Hour Psycho', Akademie der Bildende Kunste, Vienna
'...head', Uppsala Konstmuseum: Part of 'Swan-Off', Uppsala (cat.)
Galleria Bonomo, Rome: Part of the British Art Festival (cat.)
Canberra Contemporary Art Space, Canberra
Museum für Gegenwartskunst, Zurich
Galerie Walchenturm, Zurich
'Turner Prize', Tate Gallery, London

Group exhibitions (a selection)

1989
'Smith Biennial', Stirling, Scotland
'Windfall '89', Bremen (cat.)
1990
'Sites/Positions', Throughout Glasgow
'Self Conscious State', Third Eye Centre, Glasgow
(cat.)
1991
'Barclays Young Artist Award', Serpentine Gallery,
London (cat.)
'Archive project', APAC Centre d'Art Contemporain,
Nevers
'London Road...', Orpheus Gallery, Belfast
'The Bellgrove Station Billboard Project', Bellgrove,
Glasgow (cat.)
'Windfall '91', Seaman's Mission, Glasgow (cat.)
'Walk On', Jack Tilton Gallery, New York; Fruitmarket
Gallery, Edinburgh (cat.)
1992
'L'U Di Carte', Cafe Picasso, Rome
'Anomie', Patent House/Andrew Cross, London
'Speaker Project', Multiplici Culture, Rome
'A Modest Proposal', Milch Gallery, London
'Speaker Project', ICA Institute for Contemporary
Arts, London
'Love at First Sight', The Showroom, London
'And What Do You Represent?', Anthony Reynolds
Gallery, London
'Guilt By Association', The Irish Museum of Modern
Art, Dublin (cat.)
'240 Minuten', Galerie Esther Schipper, Cologne
'5 Dialogues', Museum of Natural History, Bergen,
Norway
'Instructions', Studio Marconi, Milan (cat.)
1993
'Purpose Built...', Real Art Ways, Hartford,
Connecticut
'Before The Sound Of The Beep', Artist's
soundworks throughout Paris
'Left Luggage', Maison Hanru, Paris
'Prospekt '93', Kunsthalle Frankfurt, Frankfurt (cat.)
'Douglas Gordon-Simon Patterson', Gallery
Gruppe Grün, Bremen
'Wonderful Life', Lisson Gallery, London
'Chambre 763', Hotel Carlton Palace, Paris
'High Fidelity', Kohji Ogura Gallery, Nagoya; The
Röntgen Kunst Institut, Tokyo (cat.)
1994
'WATT', Witte de With & Kunsthal, Rotterdam (cat.)
'Stains in Reality; Stan Douglas, Douglas Gordon,

Joachim Koester', Galerie Nicolai Wallner,
Copenhagen (cat.)
'Wall to Wall', Leeds City Art Gallery, Leeds, South
Bank Touring Exhibition (cat.)
'Something between my mouth and your ear',
Dolphin Gallery, Oxford. Installation for 'The
Reading Room' a project by Book Works, London
'Rue des Marins', Air de Paris, Nice
'Modern Art', Transmission Gallery, Glasgow
'Gaze: l'Impossible transparence', Carré des Arts,
Parc Floral de Paris, Paris
'Conceptual Living', Rhizome, Amsterdam
'New Painting', Chapter, Cardiff; Oriel Gallery, Mold
'Europa '94', First European Gallerist Congress,
Munich
'The Institute of Cultural Anxiety: Works from the
collection', ICA Institute of Contemporary Arts,
London (cat.)
'Some of my friends', Galerie Campbells
Occasionally, Copenhagen
'Points de vue: Images d'Europe', Centre Georges
Pompidou, Paris (cat.)
1995
'Eigen + Art: Young British Artists', Independent Art
Space, London
'Kopfbahnhof/Terminal', Hauptbahnhof Leipzig,
Leipzig (cat.)
'Take me (I'm yours)', Serpentine Gallery, London;
Kunsthalle Nürnberg, Nurnberg (cat.)
'Varje gang jag ser dig; Every Time I see You), Stora
Kvarngatan 34, Malmö; Galerie Nicolai Wallner,
Malmö
'Chez l'un, chez L'AUTRE (1)', 5 Rue des Ursulines,
Paris (cat.)
'General Release', British Council selection of
Young British Artists, Scuola di San Pasquale,
Venice (cat.)
'Shift', Foundation De Appel, Amsterdam (cat.)
'Arte Inglese d'oggi', Galleria Civica, Modena (cat.)
'Aperto '95', FRAC Languedoc-Roussillon,
Conqueyrac (cat.)
'On Board', Riva San Biagio, Venice (cat.)
'Chez l'un, chez L'AUTRE (2), 5 Rue des Ursulines,
Paris (cat.)
'Pulp Fact', Photographers' Gallery, London
'Wild Walls', Stedelijk Museum, Amsterdam (cat.)
'Am Rande der Malerei', Kunsthalle Bern, Bern
(cat.)
'Shopping', CAPC Musée d'Art Contemporain,
Bordeaux
'Korean Biennale', Kwang Jung, Korea
'Perfect Speed', MacDonald Stewart Art Center,

Guelph, Canada; Southern Florida Contemporary
Art Museum, Tampa, Florida
'Seeing Things', Galeria Antoni Estrani, Barcelona
'Biennale de Lyon', Lyon (cat.)
'The British Art Show 4', South Bank Centre,
London and Touring to Manchester, Edinburgh and
Cardiff (cat.)
  1996
'Looking Awry', Brasilian Embassy, Paris
'By Night', Fondation Cartier pour l'Art
Contemporain, Paris (cat.)
'21 Days of Darkness', Transmission Gallery,
Glasgow
'Traffic', CAPC Musée d'Art Contemporain,
Bordeaux (cat.)
'Spellbound', Hayward Gallery, London (cat.)
'Art and Film Since 1945. Hall of Mirrors', Museum
of Contemporary Art, Los Angeles; Wexner Center
for the Arts, Columbus, Ohio; Palazzo Esposizione,
Rome; Museum of Contemporary Art, Chicago
(cat.)
'Swan-Off', Uppsala Konstmuseum, Uppsala (cat.)
'Controfigura', Studio Guenzani, Milan
'Out of Space', Cole and Cole, Oxford
'Manifesta 1', Throughout Rotterdam (cat.)
'Auto reverse 2', Le Magasin Centre d'Art
Contemporain, Grenoble
'Propositions', Musée Départemental de
Rochechouart, Rochechouart (cat.)
'Nach Weimar', Kunstammlungen Weimar (cat.)
'Scream and Scream Again; Film in Art', MOMA
Museum of Modern Art, Oxford (cat.)
'Perfect', Galerie Mot & Van den Boogaard,
Brussels
'Host', OB projects, Amsterdam
'10th Sydney Biennale', Sydney (cat.)
'33 1/3', Canberra Contemporary Art Space,
Canberra (cat.)

Articles and reviews (a selection)

  1990
E. McArthur, 'Sites/Positions', *Artscribe*, No.82,
Summer, pp.77-78
  1991
L. Gillick, 'The Placebo Effect: New English art is
rooted in local reference, but makes no attempt
to aggrandize it', *Arts Magazine*, Vol.65, No.9,
May, pp.56-59
  1992
M. Archer, 'Anomie', *Art Monthly*, pp.11-13

E. Troncy, 'London Calling', *Flash Art*, Vol.25,
No.165, Summer, pp.86-89
I.C. Hunt, 'Guilt by Association', *Frieze*, No.7,
Nov-Dec, pp.48-49
  1993
T. Lawson, 'Hello, it's me', *Frieze*, No.9, March-
Apr, pp.14-17
R. Sinclair, 'Douglas Gordon: 24 Hour Psycho',
Art Monthly, No.167, June, pp.22-23
C. Henry, 'Spyhole sculpture', *The Glasgow
Herald*, Oct 15
R. Harada, 'From London', *Bijutsu Techo Monthly
Art Magazine*, Vol.45, No.678, pp.148-149
I. Buchan, 'Artist Calls the TV Shots', *The Evening
Times*, Apr 30
I. Buchan, 'Day of the Psycho', *The Evening Times*,
March 11
S. Villiers, 'Psycho with Surreal Touch', *Glasgow
Herald*, May
A. Wilson, 'Walter Benjamin's Briefcase', *Art
Monthly*, No.172, pp.30-31
  1994
J. Roberts, 'Out in the Real World', *Bijutsu Techo
Monthly Art Magazine*, Vol.46, No.688, pp.36-39
D. van den Boogerd, D. Lillington, 'It's Real But
Very Fucked Up: Een gesprek over Watt',
Metropolis M, Vol.15, No.2, Apr, pp.34-38
M. Archer, 'Collaborators', *Art Monthly*, No.178,
July-Aug, pp.3-5
'Douglas Gordon', *The Guardian*, Dec 10
C. Henry, 'A Passion That Puts Glasgow to
Shame', *The Glasgow Herald*, Dec 19
R. Cork, 'Douglas Gordon', *The Times*, Dec 31
N. Drake, 'Douglas Gordon', *The Standard*,
Dec 16
A. Wilson, 'Slowly All Around You Will Pass
Away', *Paletten*, Vol.4, No.219, pp.16-19
J. Roberts, 'Douglas Gordon', *Paletten*, Vol.4,
No.219, pp.22-25
  1995
R. Cork, 'The Naked and the Undying', *The Times*,
Jan 3
I. Blazwick, 'Douglas Gordon', *Art Monthly*,
No.183, Febr, pp.35-36
C. Henry, 'One man's Bubble Vision', *The
Glasgow Herald*, Jan 23
A. Kingston, 'Douglas Gordon', *Frieze*, No.21,
March-Apr, pp.60-61
W. Feaver, 'Douglas Gordon', *ARTnews*, Vol.94,
No.3, March, p.144
S. Murdoch, 'Dead Give-away', *Women's Art
Magazine*, No.64, May-June, pp.24-25

M. Newman, 'Beyond the Lost Object: From Sculpture to Film and Video', *Art Press*, No.202, May, pp.45-50

C. Freedman, 'Take me (I'm yours)', *Frieze*, No.23, Summer, pp.73-74

M. Maloney, 'Douglas Gordon', *Flash Art*, Vol.XXVIII, No.182, May-June, pp.114-115

M. Archer, 'Home and Away', *Art Monthly*, No.188, Jul-Aug, pp.8-10

M. Benjamin, 'Trigger happy', *British Journal of Photography*, May 17

'Les Infos du Paradis', *Parkett*, No.44, July, pp.197-201

E. Di Raddo, 'General Release', *Tema Celeste*, No.53-54, Autumn, p.88

'Agitate', *Tate Art Magazine*, No.7, Winter, p.9

R. Dorment, 'Anything but boring', *The Daily Telegraph*, Dec 30

1996

J. Fargier, 'L'immobilité hypnotique de Douglas Gordon', *Le Monde*, Jan 6

S. Moisdon-Trembley, 'Douglas Gordon, Attraction-répulsion', *Blocnotes*, No.11, Jan-Feb, pp.46-53, 109-115

M.E. Feldman, '21 Days of Darkness', *Art Monthly*, No.195, Apr, pp.38-40

'The Britsh Council Collection 1984-94', *The Art Newspaper*, Apr

'De Appel Curator League Tables', *The Crap Shooter*, No.1, Apr, p.4

J. Sans, 'Douglas Gordon: Centre Georges Pompidou', *Artforum*, Apr, pp.109-110

P. Cecchetto, 'Douglas Gordon', *Juliet*, No.77, Apr-May, pp.34-35

G. Arnason, 'What's all this talk about Glasgow?', *Siksi*, Vol.XI, No.1, Spring, pp.48-53

Y. Abriuox, 'Douglas Gordon, Pompidou Centre, Paris & Lyon Biennale', *Untitled*, No.10, Spring, pp.18-19

I. Hunt, 'Vide Video', *Art Monthly*, No.196, May, pp.3-7

J. Findlay, 'Glaswegian Goods', *Flash Art*, No.188, May-June, p.64

L. Gillick, 'The Corruption of Time', *Flash Art*, No.188, May-June, pp.69-70

L. Buck, 'Silver Scene', *Artforum*, Summer, pp.34-36

T. Jordan, 'The Glasgow boy done good', *The Scotsman*, June 24

B. Hare, 'Motion and Emotion: Walking a Tightrope', *Contemporary Art*, Vol.4, No.4, Summer, pp.42-45

C. Elwes, 'The Big Screen', *Art Monthly*, No.199, Sept, pp.11-16

S. Morgan, 'Manifesta', *Frieze*, No.30, Sept-Oct, pp.50-51

C. van Assche, 'Six questions to Douglas Gordon', *Parachute*, No.84, Oct-Dec, pp.16-19

Pubications by the artist (a selection)

1991
The Missing Text, Chance Books, London, Edited by Marysia Lewandowska

1992
'Colours for Identification...', In collaboration with Simon Patterson, *Frieze*, Vol.1, No.2, pp.14-15

1993
'Migrateurs', *Les Amis du Musée d'Art Moderne de la Ville de Paris*, Paris

'Telephone Conversation', On casette *The Speaker Project*, ICA Institute of Contemporary Arts, London

'Paris Memoires: 3 Minute Soundwork', On casette *Before The Sound Of The Beep*, Galerie Giles Peyroulet, Paris

'A Bad Trip', in cat. *Prospekt '93*, Kunsthalle Frankfurt, Frankfurt

'In Love in Vienna', *Viennese Story*, Wiener Secession, Vienna

1994
'Wall Drawing', in cat. *Wall To Wall*, Leeds City Art Gallery, Leeds

'Lost Then Found Then Lost Again', *Witte de With Cahier*, No.2, June, pp.179-183

1995
'Berlin visit', in cat. *Kopfbahnhof/Terminal*, Hauptbahnhof Leipzig, Leipzig

'2 days in spring', in cat. *On Board*, Riva San Biagio, Venice

'Grim', In collaboration with Liam Gillick, *Parkett*, No.44, pp.197-201

'Project', *Index*, No.3-4, pp.54-63

Aernout Mik

1962
Born in Groningen
Lives and works in Amsterdam

1933-1988
Academie Minerva, Groningen
1987-1988
Ateliers '63, Haarlem

Solo exhibitions (a selection)

1990
'Voorwerk', Witte de With, Rotterdam
1992
'Für Nichts und Wieder Nichts', Deweer Art
Gallery, Otegem (cat.)
'The Philosophy of Furniture', With Adam Kalkin,
Galerie Fons Welters, Amsterdam
1995
'Mommy I am sorry', With Adam Kalkin,
De Vleeshal, Middelburg
'Wie die Räume gefüllt werden müssen',
Kunstverein, Hanover
'Stuffed, Weak and Filthy', Deweer Art Gallery,
Otegem
(cat.)

Group exhibitions (a selection)

1987
'Capital Gains', 't Venster, Rotterdam
1988
'Een Grote Activiteit', Stedelijk Museum,
Amsterdam (cat.)
1989
'Mik-Leijenaar-Strik', Museum 't Kruithuis,
's-Hertogenbosch (cat.)
1990
'Capital Gains', Museum Fodor, Amsterdam
1991
'Dutch entry Biennial de São Paulo', Stedelijk Van
Abbemuseum, Eindhoven (cat.)
1993
'Recto/Verso Signalen III', ICA Institute of
Contemporay Art, Amsterdam (cat.)
Festival a/d Werf, Utrecht
'Peiling 1993', Centraal Museum, Utrecht (cat.)
1994
'Ik + de Ander', Beurs van Berlage, Amsterdam

(cat.)
'A Hundred Times', Festival a/d Werf, Utrecht
'Swallow', Museum Dhondt-Dhaenens, Deurle
'Spellbound', Centro Cultural de Belem, Lisbon;
Cruce, Madrid
'Het Zevende Museum', Stroom HCBK,
The Hague
1995
'La valise du célibatair; De koffer van de
celibatair', Railway station, Maastricht (cat.)
'A night at the show', Field, Zurich
'Wild Walls', Stedelijk Museum, Amsterdam
(cat.)
1996
'Gedraag je', Stedelijk Museum Bureau
Amsterdam, Amsterdam (Brochure)
Abendland, Munster
'Snowball', Deweer Art Gallery, Otegem (cat.)
'The Scream', Arken Museum of Modern Art,
Copenhagen
'Take 2', Centraal Museum, Utrecht (cat.)
Galerie Fons Welters, Amsterdam
'Making a place', Snug Harbor Cultural Centre,
Staten Island, New York

Articles and reviews (a selection)

1992
C. van Winkel, 'A gentle collapsing: Over de
attributen van Aernout Mik', *Metropolis M*, No.1,
pp.28-31
M. Kremer, 'Entertainment of het breekbare
geloof in een medium', *Kunst en
Museumjournaal*, No.2, pp.52-53
1993
B. Jansen, 'Aernout Mik', in cat. *De kracht van
heden*, Stichting Fonds voor Beeldende Kunsten,
Vormgeving en Bouwkunst, Amsterdam, p.198
M. Kremer, 'De wedergeboorte van het drama',
Kunst en Museumjournaal, No.2, pp.51-52
F. Hettig,' Adam Kalkin-Aernout Mik: 'The
Philosophy of Furniture', *Forum International*,
Vol.IV, No.17, March-Apr, p.125
P. Gijsberts, 'Aernout Mik en Adam Kalkin',
Metropolis M, No.1, p.50
C. van Winkel, 'Aernout Mik en Adam Kalkin: 'The
Philosophy of Furniture", *Archis*, No.3, pp.12-13
1994
M. Kremer, C. van Winkel, 'The word art, you
know, is not my primary interest: Interview with
Aernout Mik', *Archis*, No.1, pp.68-74

1995
M. Kremer, 'The life of a Repo Man is always
intense. Richard Hoeck, Aernout Mik, Joëlle
Tuerlinkx: scenario's voor een hernieuwde
bezetting van de institutionele kunstruimte',
Archis, No.6, pp.70-80.
L. Coeleweij, M. van Nieuwenhuyzen, in cat. *Wild
Walls*, Stedelijk Museum, Amsterdam
'Aernout Mik', in cat. Deweer Art Gallery, Otegem
E. Karcher, 'Aernout Mik', *Art*, No.10, Oct, p.72
1996
M. Kremer, 'Aernout Mik', *Artist Kunstmagazin*,
No.27, 2

Tony Oursler

1957
Born In New York
Lives and works in New York

1979
California Institute for the Arts

Solo exhibitions (a selection)

1981
University Art Museum, University of California,
Berkeley
'Video Viewpoints', The Museum of Modern Art,
New York
The School of the Art Institute of Chicago,
Chicago
1982
The Walker Art Center, Minneapolis
Boston Film/Video Foundation, Boston
'A Scene', P.S.1, New York
'Complete Works', The Kitchen, New York
Soho TV M/T Channel 10, New York
1983
La Mamelle, San Francisco
'My Sets', Media Study, Buffalo
'Son of Oil', A Space, Toronto
LACE-Panic House, Los Angeles Contemporary
Exhibitions, Los Angeles
'X Catholic', Performance in collaboration with
Mike Kelley, Beyond Baroque, Los Angeles
1984
Anthology Film Archives, New York
'L-7, L-5', The Kitchen, New York
1985
Kijkhuis, Den Haag
Kunst Delft, Delft
Espace Lyonnais d'Art Contemporain, Lyon
Schüle für Gestaltung, Basel
The American Center, Paris
1986
'Spheres of Influence', Centre Georges
Pompidou, Paris (cat.)
New Langton Arts, San Francisco
Nova Scotia College of Art and Design, Nova
Scotia
Boston Film/Video Foundation, Boston
1987
The Kitchen, New York

1988
'Tony Oursler's Works', Le Lieu, Quebec City
'Constellation: Intermission', Diane Brown
Gallery, New York
Western Front, Vancouver
Los Angeles Center for Photographic
Studies/EZTV, Los Angeles
1989
'Relatives', Video performance in collaboration
with Constance Dejong, The Kitchen, New York;
Rockland Center for the Arts, West Nyak; Seattle
Arts Museum, Washington; Mickery Theatre,
Amsterdam; ECG-TV Studios, Frankfurt
'Drawings, Objects, Videotapes', Delta Gallery,
Dusseldorf
Folkwang Museum, Essen (cat.)
Museum für Gegenwartskunst, Basel
Bobo Gallery, San Francisco
1990
Hallwalls, Buffalo, New York
Diane Brown Gallery, New York
The Kitchen, New York
'On Our Own', Segue Gallery, New York
1991
Diane Brown Gallery, New York
'Dummies, Hex Signs, Watercolours', The Living
Room, San Francisco
The Pacific Film Archives, San Francisco
The Cinemathèque, San Francisco
1992
'F/X Plotter, 2 Way', Kijkhuis, The Hague
'Station Project', With James Casebere, Railway
station, Kortrijk
The Space, Boston
The Knitting Factory, New York
1993
'White Trash and Phobic', Centre d'Art
Contemporain, Geneva; Kunstwerk, Berlin (cat.)
Andrea Rosen Gallery, New York
The Living Room, San Francisco
'Dummies, Dolls, and Poison Candy', Ikon
Gallery, Birmingham Bluecoat Gallery, Liverpool
(split site exhibition), (cat.)
1994
Lisson Gallery, London
Jean Bernier Gallery
Linda Cathcart Gallery, Santa Monica
'System for Dramatic Feedback', Portikus,
Frankfurt and Touring (cat.)
'Dummies, Flowers, Alters, Clouds and Organs',
Metro Pictures, New York
'Tony Oursler-Recent Video Works', The

Contemporary Art Museum, Honolulu, Hawaii
1995
Rum, Malmö
Centre d'Art Contemporain, Geneva (cat.)
'Tony Oursler: Video Installations, Objects,
Watercolors,' Musée des Arts Modernes et
Contemporains, Strassbourg (cat.)
Galerie Ghislaine Hussenot, Paris
Stedelijk Van Abbemuseum, Eindhoven (cat.)
Wiener Secession, Vienna
'Obra Reciente', Galeria Soledad Lorenzo,
Madrid (cat.)
1996
Lisson Gallery, London
Metro Pictures, New York
Museum of Contemporary Art, San Diego
(brochure)
Kasseler Kunstverein, Kassel
Jean Bernier Gallery, Athens
1997
'Judy', Institute of Contemporary Art,
Philadelphia
Margo Leavin Gallery, Los Angeles

Group exhibitions (a selection)

1984
'The Luminous Image', Stedelijk Museum,
Amsterdam (cat.)
1987
'L'époque, la mode, la morale, la passion', Centre
Georges Pompidou, Paris (cat.)
'Aspects of Media: Video', Department of Video-
Art Advisory Service of the Museum of Modern
Art for Johnson & Johnson
'Japan 1987 Television and Video Festival', Spiral,
Tokyo
'Documenta 8', Kassel (cat.)
'Schema', Baskerville + Watson Gallery, New York
1988
'The BiNational: American Art of the Late 8os,
German Art of the Late 8os', Institute of
Contemporary Art, Museum of Fine Arts, Boston
(cat.)
'Film Video Arts, 17 Years', The Museum of
Modern Art, New York
'World Wide Video Festival', The Hague (cat.)
'Twilight', Festival Belluard 88 Bolwerk, Fribourg
'2nd Videonale', Bonn (cat.)
'New York Dagen', Kunststichting, Rotterdam
'Videografia', Barcelona
'Varitish', Korea

'New York Musikk', Oslo
'Festival International du Nouveau Cinéma et de la Video', Montreal
'Replacement', LACE, Los Angeles
'Interfermental 7', Hallwalls, Buffalo
'Serious Fun Festival', Installation for Alice Tully Hall, Lincoln Center, New York

1989
'1989 Biennial Exhibition', Whitney Museum of American Art, New York (cat.)
'Video Sculpture 1963-1989', Kölnischer Kunstverein, Cologne
'Nepotism', Hallwalls, Buffalo
'Video and Language', The Museum of Modern Art, New York
'Sanity is Madness', The Artists Foundation Gallery, Boston
'World Wide Video Festival', The Hague

1990
'The Technological Muse', Katonah Museum of Art, Katonah (NY)
'Tendance Multiples, Video des Années 80', Centre Georges Pompidou, Paris (cat.)
'Video/Objects/Installations/Photography', Howard Yezerski Gallery, Boston
'Video Transforms Television: Communicating Unease', New Langton Arts, San Francisco

1991
'The New York Times Festival', Museum van Hedendaagse Kunst, Ghent
'Triune', Bluecoat Gallery, Video Positive Festival, Liverpool

1992
'Documenta 9', Kassel (cat.)

1993
'Love Again', Kunstraum Elbschloss, Elbschloss
'3rd International Biennale in Nagoya-Artec '93', Nagoya City Art Museum, Nagoya (cat.)
'Privat', Gallery F-15, Oslo

1994
'The Laugh of #12', Fort Asperen, Aquoy
Galleria Galliani, Genova
'The Figure', The Lobby Gallery, Deutsche Bank, New York
'Tony Oursler and John Kessler', Salzburger Kunstverein, Salzburg (cat.)
Metro Pictures, New York
Marian Goodman Gallery, New York
Laura Carpenter Fine Art, Santa Fe, New Mexico
'Home Video Redefined: Media Sculpture and Domesticity', Center of Contemporary Art, North Miami

'Light', ARTprop, New York
'Oh Boy, It's a Girl: Feminismen in der Kunst', Kunstverein, Munich (cat.)

1995
'ARS 95 Helsinki', Museum of Contemporary Art, Helsinki (cat.)
'The Message is the Medium: Issues of Representation in Modern Technologies', Catle Gallery, College of New Rochelle, New York
'Zeichen & Wunder', Kunsthaus Zürich, Zurich & Centro Galego de Arte Contemporanea, Santiago de Compostela (cat.)
'Festishism', Brighton Museum and Art Gallery, Brighton
'Fantastic Prayers', Collaboration with Constance Dejong and Sephen Vitiello, worldwide website project and performance, Dia Center for the Arts, Rushmore Festival, New York
'Le Printemps de Cahors', La Compagnie des Arts, Cahors
'Inside Out: Psychological Self-Portraiture', The Aldrich Museum of Contemporary Art, Connecticut (cat.)
'Trust', Tramway, Glasgow
'Face Value: American Portraits', The Parrish Art Museum, South Hampton, New York (cat.)
Mendelson Gallery, Pittsburgh
'Video Spaces: Eight Installations', The Museum of Modern Art, New York (cat.)
Metro Pictures, New York
'Man & Machine: Technology Art', Dong-Ah Gallery, Seoul
'Configura 2: Dialog Der Kulturen: Erfurt 1995', Erfurt (cat.)
'Immagini in Prospettive', Zerynthia, Rome
'L'Effet Cinéma', ARC Musée d'Art Moderne de la Ville de Paris, Paris
'1995 Carnegie International', The Carnegie Museum of Art, Pittsburgh (cat.)
'Biennale d'Art Contemporain de Lyon', Maison de Lyon, Lyon
'Passions Privé', ARC Musée d'Art Moderne de la Ville de Paris, Paris
'Playtime: Artists and Toys', Whitney Museum of American Art at Champion, Stamford (cat.)

1996
'Sampler 2', David Zwirner, New York
'Empty Dress', The Rubelle & Norman Schafler Gallery, Pratt Institute, Brooklyn
'Altered and Irrational', Whitney Museum of American Art, New York
'Sex & Crime: On Human Relationships',

Sprengel Museum, Hanover (cat.)
'Kingdom of Flora', Shoshana Wayne Gallery,
Santa Monica
'Human Technology', Revolution, Ferndale
'Young Americans: New American Art in the
Saatchi Collection', Saatchi Gallery, London (cat.)
Metro Pictures, New York
Lisson Gallery, London
'Tomorrow', Rockland Center for the Arts, West
Nyack (NY)
The Cincinnatti Art Museum, Cincinnatti
'New York 'Unplugged II'', Gallery Cotthem,
Knokke-Zoute
'Phantasmagoria', Museum of Contemporary
Art, Sydney (cat.)
Metro Pictures, New York
'Radical Images: 2nd Austrian Triennial on
Photography 1996', Neue Galerie am Landes-
museum Joanneum, Graz; Camera Austria in the
Kunsthalle Szombathely (cat.)
'Scream & Scream Again: Film in Art', MOMA
Museum of Modern Art, Oxford (cat.)
10th Biennale of Sydney, Sydney (cat.)
'Matthew Barney, Tony Oursler, Jeff Wall',
Sammlung Goetz, Munich (cat.)
'Being & Time: The Emergence of Video
Projection', The Albright-Knox Art Gallery, Buffalo
'New Persona; New Universe', Biennale di
Firenze, Florence
Philadelphia Museum of Art, Philadelphia,
Performance with Constance Dejong
'The Red Gate', Whitney Museum of American
Art, New York
Museum of Contemporary Art, Ghent
'The Scream', The Nordic Arts Centre, Helsinki

Articles and reviews (a selection)

1982
J. Hoberman, 'The Weak Bullet, The Loner: Grand
Mal', *The Village Voice*, March 23
1983
R. Atkins, 'Chicago', *Artforum*, Apr
1984
A. Zeichner, 'Critique of Pure Reason', *The Village
Voice*, Apr 3
1985
K. Gordon, 'American Prayers', *Artforum*, pp.73-
77
A. Wooster, 'Tony Oursler at MO David', *Art in
America*, Dec

1986
D. Lalanne, 'Tony Oursler: Dernier Soir', *Cinéma*,
Febr, p.380
1987
J. Fargier, 'Installation a Beaubourg', *Le Journal
Cahiers du Cinéma*, Febr, p.380
1988
J. Berlinsky, 'The Light Fantastic', *Metro*, Oct
J. Hohmeyer, 'Die Fernbedienung der
Kunstgeschichte', *Der Spiegel*, p.52
E. Sage, 'The Joy of Collaboration: An Interview
with Constance Dejong and Tony Oursler',
Vancouver Guide, p.4
1989
C. Carr, 'Constance Dejong and Tony Oursler:
Relatives, The Kitchen', *Artforum*, May, p.27
C. Hagen, 'Video Art: The Fabulous Chameleon',
ARTnews, Summer, p.88
R. Lange, 'Media Power: Video-Arbeiten von Tony
Oursler', *Apex-Heft*, p.70
M. Tiberio, 'Method to this Media: An Interview
with Tony Oursler', *Visions, a publication for the
media arts by the Boston Film/Video Foundation*,
Summer, p.3
M. Blowen, 'A Stunning Mix of Images and
Words at ICA', *The Boston Globe*
1990
J. Lintinen, 'Uudella Mediataiteella Taitaa Olla
Halussaan 90-luvun Avaiment' (To Break into the
New Media Arts is to Possess the Key to the
1990 s), *Taide*, p.2
A. Grundberg, 'Review/Photography: Tony
Oursler, Diane Brown Gallery', *The New York
Times*, June 8
A. Taubin, 'Choices', *The Village Voice*, June 20
D. Hall & S.J. Fifer (eds.), *Illuminating Video: An
Essential Guide to Video Art*, Aperture Foundation,
New York
D. Joselit, 'Mind Over Matter: Tony Oursler and
Ericka Beckman Master the Politics of Art', *The
Boston Phoenix*, Sept 7
J. Decter, 'Tony Oursler: Diane Brown Gallery',
Arts Magazine, Oct, p.65
J. Miller, 'Tony Oursler: Diane Brown Gallery',
Artforum, Oct, p.29
1991
T. Labat, 'Tony Oursler', *Shift*, p.5
H. Mackey, 'Something Fishy Going On', *After
Dark*, Febr
1992
P. Iden, 'Trotz Grosser Fulle sehr, sehr Wenig',
Frankfurter Rundschau, June 13

A.G. Artner, 'Matter Over Mind', *The Chicago Tribune*, June 28
R. Cornwell, 'Great Videos, Shame About the Show', *Art Monthly*, Sept
Y. Ramirez, 'Diane Brown Gallery', *Art in America*, May

1993
S. Sarrazin, 'Tony Oursler en de nieuwe gedaante van de videokunst', *Metropolis M*, p.6
C. Meigh-Andrews, 'Tony Oursler', *Art Monthly*, Nov
A. Taubin, 'The Big Sleep', *The Village Voice*, Aug 3
G. Sandquist, 'Privat', *Parkett*

1994
W. Januszczak, 'Heart of the Matter', *The New York Times*, Febr 27
S. Kent, 'Dummy Copy', *Time Out*, Febr 16
C. Henderson, 'Household items star in art show', *The Miami Herald*, Febr 6
H.L. Kohen, 'Home video never looked like this', *The Miami Herald*
G. Norman, 'Saatchi Swoops for Video Pieces', *The London Times*, Febr
R. Dorment, 'Portraits for the Age of Anxiety', *The Daily Telegraph*
K. Levin, 'Trans-Europe Express', *The Village Voice*, Sept 27, p.94
C. McCormick, 'True Terror', *Paper*, Nov, p.31
E. Janus, 'Sue Williams, Renee Green, Tony Oursler', *Furor* (Voltaire), Sept, No.26
R. Puvogel, 'Tony Oursler-System for Dramatic Feedback', *Kunstforum*, Nov, pp.403-404
R. Schmitz, 'Frankfurt: Tony Oursler im Portikus', *Kunstbulletin*, Oct, p.39
L. Geerling, 'De lach van de gehangene', *Metropolis M*, No.4, pp.34-39
D. Pieters, 'Het geheim achter het lachen', *NRC Handelsblad*, Oct 6
M. van der Jagt, 'Reis van onder naar bovenlichaam', *De Groene Amsterdammer*, June 15
M. Pesch, 'Tony Ourslers Videoskulputuren in Frankfurt: Mehr als Medien Feedback', *Frankfurt Neue Presse (Die Tageszeitung)*, Sept 30
GN, 'Der Betrachter wird selber zum Objekt', *Frankfurter Neue Presse (Die Tageszeitung)*, Aug 27
GN, 'Der Mensch von heute schreit sein Angst heraus', *Frankfurter Neue Presse (Die Tageszeitung)*
D. Baer-Bogenschutz, 'Beobachter der Beobachter', *Frankfurter Rundschau*, Sept 22
P. Schjeldahl, 'Get Out of Here', *The Village Voice*, Nov 25, p.97

R. Smith, 'Tony Oursler', *The New York Times*, Nov 25, p.C24
J. Heiser, 'Den Plot ernst nehmet: Tony Ourslers Installation 'System for Dramatic Feedback'', *Texte zur Kunst*, Vol.4, No.16, Nov., pp.191-194
A. Spiegel, 'John Kessler-Tony Oursler', *Arti*, Vol.22, Nov-Dec, pp.208-211

1995
M. Schwendener, 'Tony Oursler: Dummies, Flowers, Alters, Clouds and Organs', *Art Papers*, Jan-Febr, p.59
M. Duncan, 'Tony Oursler at Metro Pictures', *Art in America*, Vol.83, No.1, Jan, p.105
J. Decter, 'Tony Oursler: Metro Pictures', *Artforum*, Vol.XXXIII, No.6, Febr, p.89
G. Volk, 'Tony Oursler: Metro Pictures', *ARTnews*, Febr, p.127
R. Edelman, 'Tony Oursler', *Art Press*, No.199, Febr, pp.VI-VII
I. Bratschi, 'Tony Oursler Parvient à Faire Parler d'Étranges Poupées', *Le Courrier*, Geneva, Feb 3
M.P. Druey, 'L'Americain Oursler Hurle à Geneve', *Tribune des Arts*, March, p.15
Tony Oursler, 'Why I Like Flowers', *Paletten*, March, pp.30-33
J.P.F., 'Tony Oursler', *Le Monde*, March 19-20
C. Vogel, 'Inside Art', *The New York Times*, April 7
J.C. Welchman, 'Tony Oursler: Angels of the Techno-Grotesque', *Art + Text*, No.51, May, pp.25-27
C. 'Back in Fashion: Video Installations', *The New York Times*, July 11, pp.C-13, C-15
G. Glueck, 'Turn On, Tune In and Drop By: Video Art's Come a Long Way', *The New York Observer*, July 24, p.20
J. Russell, 'Portraits That Beckon To the Cross-Examiner', *The New York Times*, Aug 11, p.C30
D. Colman, 'The Art Screen Scene', *Artforum*, Vol.XXXIV, No.2, Sept, pp.9-10
A.C. Dano, 'Art: TV and Video', *The Nation*, Sept 11, pp.248-253
E. Heartney, 'Video in City', *Art in America*, Oct, pp.94-99
J. Lewis, 'Doll Parts', *Spin*, Nov, p.28
M. Ritchie, 'Video Spaces: Eight Installations, MOMA', *Zingmagazine*, Autumn
G. Czöppan, 'Künstler des Jahres', *Focus*, Oct, pp.146-150
E. Licata, 'Living With Art', *ARTnews*, Dec, pp.87-90

1996
R. Smith, 'A Neo-Surrealist Show With a

Revisionist Agenda', *The New York Times*, Jan 12,
p.C23
W. Zimmer, 'No Simple Innocence, Childhood
Now Invoked Has More in Tow', *The New York
Times*, Jan 21, p.CN16
M. Ritchie, 'Tony Oursler: Technology As An
Instinct Amplifier', *Flash Art*, Jan-Feb, pp.76-79
S. Kandel', 'Kingdom of Flora' Blooms Again', *Los
Angeles Times*, Febr 22, pp.F3, F12
L. Berke, 'Short Bytes: Kingdom of Flora', *Los
Angeles Jewish Times*, March 15
M. Herbert, 'Project Yourself Onto This: Interview',
Dazed & Confused, Apr, pp.102-104
H. Halle, 'The Vision Thing', *Time Out New York*,
May 1-8, p.22
L. Camhi, 'A Sharpie's Crisis', *The Village Voice*,
May 7, pp.79-80
M. Maloney, 'Young Americans: Parts I & II',
Flash Art, May-June, pp.108-109
R. Ehmke, ed., with E. Licata, 'Consider the
Alternatives: 20 Years of Contemporary Art at
Hallwalls', Hallwalls Inc., Buffalo
'Tony Oursler', *The New Yorker*, May 20, pp.16-17
S. Ward, 'Tony Oursler at Metro Pictures: Review',
Art in Context, web site
H. Cotter, 'Optic Nerve', *Art in America*, Vol.83,
No.6, June, pp.92-95
Y. Kaoru, 'Tony Oursler', *BT*, Vol.48, No.726,
June, pp.53-59
D. Batchelor, 'Tony Oursler: Lisson Gallery',
Artforum, Vol.XXXIV, No.10, Summer, p.118
S. Ward, 'Tony Oursler', *Art in Context*, web site,
May 17
L. Ollmann, 'Art That Talks Back: The Shrink Is
In', *Los Angeles Times*, Calendar Section, June 30,
pp.55-56
C. James, 'Art Flickers From Video Screens', *The
New York Times*, July 26, pp.C1, C4
'Tony Oursler', A written conversation with C.
Meyer-Stoll and J. Lewis, Museum of
Contemporary Art, San Diego (brochure)
C. Andres, 'Tony Oursler: Review', *Katalog*,
Denmark, Autumn, p.50
T. Hummer, 'Tony Oursler: Review', *Sculpture*,
Sept, pp.63-64
Collaboration Tony Oursler, Raymond Pettibon,
Thomas Schütte, *Parkett*, No.47, Sept

Publications by the artist (a selection)

1987
'Phototrophic' in *Forehead BD*

1988
'Vampire', *Communications Video*, Nov, p.48
1990
'Phototrophic', *Illumination Video: An Essential
Guide to Video Art*, D. Hall, S.J. Fifer (eds.),
Aperture Foundation, New York
1991
'Triune: A Work in Progress', *Visions*, Summer, p.5
1995
'Dummies', Flowers, and Altars' (portfolio),
Grand Street: Games, J. Stein (ed.), Jean Stein &
Torsten Weisel, New York
'The Warped Vision of Bruce Nauman', *Paper*,
May

Sam Samore

Lives and works in New York

Solo exhibitions (a selection)

1988
American Fine Arts Co., New York
1990
Galerie Bleich-Rossi, Graz
American Fine Arts Co., New York
1991
Galerie Christian Nagel, Cologne
Nordanstad-Skarstedt Galerie, Stockholm
Luhring Augustine Hetzler Gallery, Santa Monica
1992
Galerie Marc Jancou, Zurich
Galleria Massimo De Carlo, Milan
1994
Galerie Anne de Villepoix, Paris
'Tangled Web of Erotic Savage Cunning',
De Appel Foundation, Amsterdam (cat.)
'Situations', Kunsthalle Zürich, Zurich (cat.)
Marc Jancou Gallery, London
1995
Thomas Nordanstad Gallery, New York
'Allegories of Beauty', Galerie Borgmann
Capitain, Cologne
Kunstverein Elsterpark, Leipzig
1996
Richard Telles Gallery, Los Angeles
'Allegories of Beauty (incomplete)', DAAD
Galerie, Berlin
'Allegories of Beauty (incomplete)', Galleria
Massimo De Carlo, Milan
'Allegories of Beauty (incomplete)', Galerie Anne
de Villepoix, Paris
'Scenarios', Thomas Nordanstad Gallery, New
York

Group exhibitions (a selection)

1990
'Stephen Prina, Sam Samore, Christopher Wool',
Galerie Schurr, Stuttgart
'Cady Noland, Sam Samore, Karen Sylvester',
Galerie Max Hetzler, Cologne (cat.)
'Sam Samore, Lawrence Weiner', Air de Paris,
Nice
1991
'Kirsten Mosher, Sam Samore, Beat Streuli',

Galerie Anne de Villepoix, Paris
'Le Revanche de l'Image', Galerie Pierre Huber,
Geneva (cat.)
'The Museum of Natural History', Barbara Farber
Gallery, Amsterdam (cat.)
1992
'Paysages dans une Ruine Potentielle', 19th
Arrondissement, Paris
'1968', Le Consortium, Dijon
'Tableaux Volés', Sylvana Lorenz Gallery, Paris
'In Through the Out Door', Nordanstad-
Skarstedt Gallery, New York
'Anomie', Patent House, London
'Spielhölle', University of Frankfurt Metro
Station, Frankfurt (cat.)
'Still', Andrea Rosen Gallery, New York
'The Big Nothing (or le Presque Rien)', The New
Museum of Contemporary Art, New York (cat.)
'Through the View Finder', De Appel Foundation,
Amsterdam (cat.)
'Exhibit A', Serpentine Gallery, London (cat.)
'Writing on the Wall', 303 Gallery, New York
'Twenty Fragile Pieces', Galerie Analix, Geneva
(cat.)
1993
American Fine Arts Co., New York
'The Young Americans', Galerie Sophia Ungers,
Cologne
'Live in your Head', Institut für Museumskunde,
Hochschule für Angewandte Kunst, Vienna
'Travelogue-Reisetagebuch', Institut für
Museumskunde, Hochschule für Angewandte
Kunst, Vienna (cat.)
'Spielhölle', Sylvana Lorenz Gallery, Paris (cat.)
'Entrevues', Ars Musica, Brussels (cat.)
'Serial', Zurich (cat.)
'Time and Tide', Tyne International 1993,
Newcastle (cat.)
'Avant le Bip Sonore', Galerie Anne de Villepoix,
Paris (audiocassette)
David Zwirner Gallery, New York
'Restaurant', La Bocca, Paris
'Open Ditch', Hôpital Ephémère, Paris
'Centre Paris/Zentrum Paris', Kunsthalle Ritter,
Klagenfurt (cat.)
'Viennese Story', Wiener Secession, Vienna (cat.)
1994
'Die zweite Wirklichkeit', Schloss Wilhelm,
Stuttgart
'Pictures of the Real World (in Real Time)', Paula
Cooper Gallery, New York (cat.)
'F & S Universal-Come Together Edition', Les

Entrepôts Laydet, Paris
'Rock My World', Independent Art Space, London (cat.)
'Gaze: The Impossible Transparence', Carré des Arts, Parc Floral, Paris (cat.)
'PlayOff', Art & Public, Geneva
'Martin Creed, Sam Samore', Marc Jancou Gallery, London
'Sur la route, entre Besançon et Belfort: Voyage épique', Centre d'Art Mobile, Besançon (video cassette)
'Pictures of the Real World', Le Consortium, Dijon
'Heart of Darkness', Kröller-Müller Museum, Otterlo (cat.)
'The Use of Pleasure', Terrain, San Francisco (cat.)
    1995
'The Peace Process, The Magic Bed', Ferens Art Gallery, Hull (cat.)
'Pièces Meublées', Galerie Jousse Seguin, Paris
'Stoppage', CCC Tours, France
'On Board', Venice Biennale, Venice (cat.)
'Shopping', CAPC Musée d'Art Moderne, Bordeaux (cat.)
'26ème Rencontres Internationales de la Photographie', Arles
'Infra-sound', Künstlerhaus Hamburg, Hamburg (cat.)
'Morceaux choisis', Le Magasin Centre d'Art Contemporain, Grenoble (cat.)
'Pictures of the Real World (in Real Time)', Galleria Massimo De Carlo, Milan
'Situations', Forum Stadtpark, Graz (cat.)
'Filmcuts', Galerie Neuger Riemschneider, Berlin
'Campo', Venice Biennale, Venice (cat.)
'The Young Americans', Galerie Sophia Ungers, Cologne
'The Stranger', David Zwirner Gallery, New York
'Pictures of the Real World (in Real Time)', Hara Museum of Contemporary Art, Tokyo (cat.)
    1996
Grande Galerie, École Régionale des Beaux-Arts, Rouen
'Sugar Hiccup: Elizabeth Ballet, Richard Wright, Sam Samore', Tramway, Glasgow (cat.)
'C'est arrivé près de chez nous', FRAC Haute Normandie, Galerie Marcel Duchamp, Yvetôt
'Tableaux de la Vie Moderne', Galerie Rodolphe Janssen, Brussels
'The quiet in the land', The Shaker Museum, Shaker Village; Sabbathday Lake, Maine, Plaq

'Many True Stories', Bergkerk, Deventer (cat.)
'Modèles corrigés', Collège Marcel Duchamp, Châteauroux (cat.)
'Les Contes de fées se terminent bien', FRAC Haute Normandie, Château de Val Ferneuse, Sotteville-sous-le-Val (cat.)

Interventions

    1993
'Nu et Habillé', Cabaret au Pigall's, Paris
    1994
'F & S Universal-Come Together Edition', Les Entrepôts Laydet, Paris
'Nu et Habillé 2', Cabaret au Pigall's, Paris
'Tube', TeleTube Video Fun Presentation, Hôpital Ephémère, Paris

Georgina Starr

1968
Born in Leeds
Lives and works in London

1987-1989
Middlesex Polytechnic, Middlesex
1990-1992
Slade School of Art, London

Fellowships and awards

1992
British Institute Award Sculpture
Duveen Travel Award
1993-1994
Rijksacademie van Beeldende Kunst, Amsterdam
1993
VSB Bank Award
Leverhulme Trust Award
Urlot Prize

Solo exhibitions (a selection)

1992
'Mentioning', Anthony Reynolds Gallery, London
1994
'Getting to Know You', Anthony Reynolds Gallery, London
'(Un)Controlling', Stedelijk Museum Bureau Amsterdam, Amsterdam (brochure)
'The Nine Collections of the Seventh Museum', Stroom HCBK, The Hague
'Crying', Galerie Krinzinger, Vienna
1995
'Visit to a Small Planet', Kunsthalle Zürich, Zurich
Rooseum, Center of Contemporary Arts, Malmö
'The Party', Bloom Gallery, Amsterdam
1996
'Hypnodreamdruff: Art Now', Tate Gallery, London
Barbara Gladstone Gallery, New York

Group exhibitions (a selection)

1990
Mall Galleries, London
'A.V.E. 90', Gemeente Museum, Arnhem
1991
'A.V.E. 91', Filmhuis, Arnhem
1992
'P.G.6', Slade Gallery, London
'Through View', Diorama Gallery, London
1993
'Barclays Young Artists', Serpentine Gallery, London (cat.)
'Aperto', Venice Biennale, Venice (cat.)
'Ha-Ha', Killerton House, Devon (cat.)
'Wonderful Life', Lisson Gallery, London
'Restaurant', La Bocca, Paris
'High Fidelity', Kohji Ogura Gallery, Nagoya; The Röntgen Kunst Institut, Tokyo (cat.)
'Open Atelierdagen', Rijksacademie, Amsterdam
1994
Andrea Rosen Gallery, New York
'Looking at Words: Reading Pictures', Eilms Lester, London and Touring
'Without Walls', The Face Magazine
'WM Karaoke', Portikus, Frankfurt
'Europa 94', Munich
'Untitled Streamer Eddy Monkey Full Stop Etcetera', Anthony Reynolds Gallery, London
'Le Shuttle', Künstlerhaus Bethanien, Berlin (cat.)
Schipper & Krome, Cologne
'Electric Ladyland', Jousse Seguin, Paris
'Points de vue (Images d'Europe)', Centre Georges Pompidou, Paris (cat.)
'Use Your Allusion: Recent Video Art', Museum of Contemporary Art, Chicago (cat.)
'It's how you play the game', Exit Art, New York
1995
Kunstforeningen, Copenhagen
Anthony Reynolds Gallery, London
'Hopeless', Center for Contemporary Art, Glasgow
'In Search of the Miraculous', Starkmann Ltd., London
'Everytime I See You', Malmö, (Nicolai Wallner)
'La valise du célibataire; De koffer van de celibatair', Railway station, Maastricht (cat.)
'Couldn't get ahead', Independent Art Space, London
'Auto Reverse', Saint Gervais, Geneva
'Wild Walls', Stedelijk Museum, Amsterdam (cat.)

'Ateliers d'Artistes de la Ville de Marseille',
Marseilles
'Night and Day', Anthony Reynolds Gallery,
London
''Brilliant!', New Art from London', Walker Art
Center, Minneapolis (cat.)
'Brill', Montgomerie Glasoe Fine Art,
Minneapolis
'Troisième Biennale de Lyon', Lyon (cat.)
'The British Art Show 4', South Bank Centre,
London and Touring to Manchester, Edinburgh
and Cardiff (cat.)
1996
'No10', Rhona Hoffman Gallery, Chicago
'The Cauldron', DeanClough, Henry Moore
Institute, Halifax (cat.)
'Elsewhere', Galerie Froment Putman, Paris
Roslyn Oxley Gallery, Sydney
'Art & Video in Europe: Electronic
Undercurrents', Statens Museum for Kunst,
Copenhagen (cat.)
Ferens Art Gallery, Kingston upon Hull
'Fernbedienung', Grazer Kunstverein, Graz
'New Photography 12', Museum of Modern Art,
New York
'Full House', Kunstmuseum Wolfsburg,
Wolfsburg

Articles and reviews (a selection)

1993
D. Alberge, *The Independent*, Jan 27
F. Whitford, 'Blind Man's Bluff', *The Sunday
Times*, Jan 31
T. Hilton, 'Familar Signs of a Misspent Youth',
The Independent on Sunday, Feb 7
S. Grant, 'Review', *City Limits*, Feb 25
J. Roberts, 'Twins Peak', *Frieze*, No.9, Mar-Apr
D. Lillington, 'Treu Brit', *Time Out*, July 8
R. Shone, 'God's bods and odd bods', *The
Observer*, Aug 8
G. Norman, 'Creations to turn the critics purple',
The Independent, Aug 9
A. Wilson, 'Ha-Ha and Over the Limit', *Art
Monthly*, Sept
L. Cottingham, 'Wonderful Life', *Frieze*, No.12,
Sept-Oct
G. Muir, 'Yesterday', *Frieze*, No.13, Nov-Dec
R. Steenbergen, 'Grote diversiteit op Open
Atelierdagen van Rijksacademie', *NRC
Handelsblad*, Dec 13
D. Mellor, 'Wonderful Life', *Untitled Winter*

1994
K. Eshun, 'The Rising Stars of 94'', *I-D magazine*,
No.125, Feb
J. Roberts, 'Georgina Starr: Andere stemmen',
Metropolis M, Vol.15, No.1, Feb, pp.32-33
D. Alberge, 'Arts Centre show is not for the
camera-shy', *The Independent*, Feb 5
I. Schwartz, 'Schijnbare orde van de wereld', *De
Volkskrant*, March 4
M. Gibbs, '(Un)Controlling', *Art Monthly*, No.175,
Apr, pp.25-26
J. Roberts, 'The Up and Coming London Art
Scene', *Bijutsu Techo Monthly Art Magazine*,
Vol.46, No.688
A. Choon, 'Taking Roads Less Traveled', *Art &
Antiques*, May
A. Renton, 'Georgia Starr', *Flash Art*, Vol.27,
No.176, June, p.120
A. Leturcq, 'Georgina Starr', *Blocnotes*, No.6,
Summer
S. Grant, 'World Cup Football Karaoke', *Art
Monthly*, No.179, Sept, p.37
K. Bernard, 'Art Mart', Oct
M. Williams, 'Starr Turn', *Vogue*, Oct
1995
J. Ferguson, 'Starr of the future', *The Observer
Review*, Jan 1
T. Corvi Mora, 'Georgina Starr', *Purple Prose*,
Spring
A. Russo, 'A Body of Works', *Art Monthly*, No.185,
Apr, pp. 24-25
D. Dandurand, 'Is Georgina a Starr?', *Technikart*,
March-Apr, p.36
L. Bovier, 'Irrepressible Narcissisme', *Tribune de
Genève*, May 5
P. Régnier, 'Georgina Starr', *Blocnotes*, Summer,
No.9, p.81
S. Laybourne, 'A Bush With Style', *The Daily
Telegraph*, July 17, p.15
S. van der Meulen, 'Wild Walls', *Metropolis M*,
No.5, pp. 40-41
R. Pontzen, 'De Sixties zijn ook terug in het
Stedelijk', *Vrij Nederland*, Sept 30
R. Flood, 'Smashing', *Frieze*, No.25, pp.32-36
A. Bangma, 'Wild Walls', *Frieze*, No.25, pp.61-62
S. Corrigan, 'New Art Riot', *I.D. magazine*, Dec, p.39
'What do the Stars Want for Christmas?', *The
Guardian*, Dec 16
R. Garnett, 'The British Art Show 4', *Art Monthly*,
No.192, Dec-Jan, pp.27-29
1996
A. Chodzko, 'Georgina Starr: Interview', *Tate The*

Art Magazine, Spring, pp.34-39
H. Reitmaier, 'Things You Always Wanted to Do but Were Afraid to: Interview', *Women's Art Magazine*, Jan-Feb, pp.12-15
T. Guha, 'Weird Science', *The Face*, Feb, p.28
C. Lyttelton, 'Artist of the month: Georgina Starr', *Tatler*, Feb, p.18
E. Windsor, 'Bright Young Thing', *Dazed and Confused*, No.17, p.18
S. Kent, 'Knowing Me, Knowing You', *Time Out*, Feb 7-14, pp.16-17
L. Corner, 'Now You See Me', *The Big Issue*, Feb 19-25
M. Gayford, 'Artist with a future in light Entertainment', *The Daily Telegraph*, Feb 21
'Georgina Starr on Paul McCarthy's Pinocchio Nose-Pipe', *The Guardian*, Apr 2
R. Thoburn, 'Hypnodreamdruff', *Trash*, No.1
R. Stone, 'Feds, Thieves and Grasses', *Women's Art Magazine*, Aug-Sept, pp.30-31
A. Leturcq, 'Georgina Starr, The Perfect Party: Interview', *Blocnotes*, pp.26-36
F. Hünter, 'Die Enkel der Infizierten', *Kleine Zeitung*, p.57
S. Rifbjerg, 'Strom Pa', *Kultur*, Sept 6-12

Gillian Wearing

1963
Born in Birmingham
Lives and works in London

1987-1990
Goldsmiths' College, University of London, London
1985-1987
Chelsea School of Art

Awards

1993
BT Young Contemporaries

Solo exhibitions (a selection)

1993
City Racing, London
1994
Interim Art, London
1995
'Western Security', Hayward Gallery, London
1996
'Wish You Were Here', Video evenings at De Appel Foundation, Amsterdam
Le Consortium, Dijon
'City Projects: Prague, Part II', The British Council, Prague, Valentina Moncada, Rome
Interim Art, London

Group exhibitions (a selection)

1991
'Piece Talks', Diorama Art Centre, London
'Clove 1', The Clove Building, London
'Empty Gestures', Diorama Art Centre, London
1992
'Instruction', Galleria Marconi, Milan
'British Art Group Show', Le Musée des Beaux Arts, Le Havre
1993
'BT Young Contemporaries', Cornerhouse, Manchester; Orchard Gallery, Derry; The Maplin Art Gallery, Sheffield; City Museum and Art Gallery, Stoke-on-Trent; Centre for Contemporary Art, Glasgow
'Okay Behaviour', 303 Gallery, New York
'Mandy Loves Declan 100%', Mark Boote Gallery,

New York
'2 into 1', Centre 181 Gallery, London
'Vox Pop', Laure Genillard Gallery, London
1994
'Le Shuttle', Künstlerhaus Bethanien, Berlin (cat.)
'3.016.026', Theoretical Events, Naples
'Uncertain Identity', Galerie Analix B & L Polla, Geneva
'Fuori Fase', Via Farini, Milan
'Domestic Violence', Gio Marconi's House, Milan
'R.A.S.', Galerie Analix B & L. Polla, Geneva
'Not Self-Portrait', Karsten Schubert, London
1995
'X/Y', Centre Georges Pompidou, Paris
'Campo', Venice Biennale, Venice (cat.)
'Sage', Galerie Michel Rien, Tours
'It's not a picture', Galleria Emi Fontana, Milan
''Brillant!', New Art from London', Walker Art Center, Minneapolis; (cat.)
'The British Art Show 4', South Bank Centre, London and Touring to Manchester, Edinburgh and Cardiff (cat.)
'Mysterium Alltag', Kampnagel, Hamburg
'Aperto '95', Le Nouveau Musée, Institut d'Art Contemporain, Villeurbanne (cat.)
'Hotel Mama: Aperto '95', Kunstraum Wien, Vienna
'Make Believe', Royal College of Art, London
'Mobius Strip', Basilico Fine Arts, New York
'Hello!', Andréhn-Schiptjenko, Stockholm
'Gone, Blum & Poe', Los Angeles
1996
'Life/Live', ARC Musée d'Art Moderne de la Ville de Paris, Paris (cat.)
'Full House: Young British Art', Kunstmuseum Wolfsburg, Wolfsburg (cat.)
'Playpen & Corpus Delirium', Kunsthalle Zürich, Zurich (cat.)
'A/Drift: Scenes From the Penetrable Culture', Center for Curatorial Studies, Bard College, New York (cat.)
'The Aggression of Beauty', Galerie Arndt & Partner, Berlin
'Electronic Undercurrents: Art & Video in Europe', The Royal Museum of Fine Arts, Copenhagen
'Private View, Contemporary Art in the Bowes Museum', Barnard Castle, County Durham, Organized by the Henry Moore Institute, Halifax
'The Fifth New York Video Festival', The Film Society of Lincoln Center, New York

'Toyama Now '96', The Museum of Modern Art, Toyama
'The Cauldron', Dean Clough, Henry Moore Institute, Halifax (cat.)
'NowHere', Louisiana Museum of Modern Art, Humlebaek (cat.)
'Auto-reverse 2', Le Magasin Centre National d'Art Contemporain, Grenoble
'Imagined Communities', Oldham Art Gallery, John Hansard Gallery, Southampton; Firstsite, Colchester; Walsall Museum & Art Gallery; Royal Festival Hall, London; Gallery of Modern Art, Glasgow
'Pandaemonium: London Festival of Moving Images', ICA Institute of Contemporary Arts, London
'Traffic', CAPC Musée d'Art Contemporain, Bordeaux (cat.)

Articles and reviews

1991
CV Journal, Paris
1992
'Hype', *The Face*, No.51, Dec
The Independent on Sunday, Dec 27
1993
W. Feaver, 'Treasures in the Wendy House of the Lost Boys', *The Observer*, July 4
T. Guha, *Time Out*
M. Archer, 'O Camera O Mores', *Art Monthly*
J. Stallabass, 'Power to the People', *Art Monthly*
A. Graham-Dixon, 'That Way Madness Lies', *The Independent*
C. Milner, 'Positive Exposure for New Talent', *The Saturday Times*
1994
D. Lillington, 'Real Life in London', *Paletten*, No.219, Apr, p.12
A. Searle, *Frieze*, No.18, Sept-Oct, pp.61-62
G. Muir, *World Art Magazine*, Inaugural U.S. Edition, Nov, p.117
M. Jaio, 'Cinco Artistas Inglesas: Voces En El Espacio', *Lapiz*, No.106, Oct-Nov, pp.12-1
M. Currah, *Time Out*, No.1245, June 29-July 6, p.50
S. Craddock, *The Times*, June 14
J. Savage, 'Vital Signs', *Artforum*, March, pp.60-63
K. Bush, 'Vox Pop', *Untitled*, London
Harpers Magazine, Vol.288, No.1728, p.21
A. Searle, 'Vox Pop', *Time Out*, Jan 5-12, p.42

1995

W. Januzczak, 'Cool Britannia', *The Sunday Times*, Culture Section, Dec 3

'These are the Rising Stars of 96', *The Independent*, Weekend Section, Dec 30

R. Cork, 'Forthcoming Attractions', *The Times Magazine on Saturday*, Nov 18

S. Corrigan, 'Get the Picture, Britsh Art's Next Superstars', *I-D magazine*, Dec

J. Kastner, 'Brilliant', *Art Monthly*, Dec-Jan

C. Tomkins, 'London Calling', *The New Yorker*, Dec 11, pp.115-117

R. Smith, 'Some British Moderns Seeking to Shock', *The New York Times*, Dec

L. MacRithchie, 'Shock Artists', *The Financial Times*, Nov 17

A. Patrizio, 'Hayward Shoot Out', *Gallery Guide*, Sept

J. Hall, 'Butterfly Ball', *The Guardian*, Nov 14

A. Searle, 'British Art with Attitude', *The Independent*, Nov 14

W. Feaver, 'Where Theres a Wilt....', *Observer Review*, Nov 19

D. Barrat, 'Hayward Gallery', *Art Monthly*, Nov

M. Gayford, 'Youth, formaldehyde and the spirit of the age', *The Telegraph Magazine*, Nov 11

M. Currah, 'Group Show: Interim Art', *Time Out*, Oct 11

J. Morrish, 'Wildlife: Martyrs to their art', *The Telegraph Magazine*, Oct 7

A. Searle, 'Faces to Watch In The Art World', *The Independent*, Sept 26

J. Hall, 'Western Security', *The Guardina*, Sept

M. Currah, 'Action Replayed', *Time Out*, Sept 20

W. Harvey, 'Bodies of Work', *The Observer Life Magazine*, Sept 9

D. Cavendish, 'Gallery Gunslingers on a Shoot to Thrill', *The Independent*, Sept 11

G. Wearing, 'Hommage to the Woman with the Bandaged Face who I saw Yesterday Down Walworth Road', *Blocnotes*, No.9, pp.18-19

G. Wearing, 'A Short Love Story', *Nummer 3*, Sept, p.81

P. Bonaventura, 'Profile: Wearing Well', *Art Monthly*, No.184, March, pp.24-26

C. Faure Walker, 'Signs of the Times', *Creative Camera*, Feb-March, pp.34-37

C. Landesman, S. Rogers, 'Talking Pictures', *The Big Issue*, No.116, Febr, pp.12-14

S. Kent, 'Make Believe', *Time Out*, Feb-March, p.46

'British Art: Don't Knock It', *The Independent*, Weekend Section, June 24, p.1 & 4

1996

'Artisti Britannici a Roma', Umberto Allemandi & C, Torino

R. Shone, 'Made in London', Simmons & Simmons International Law Firm, London

G. Muir , 'Gillian Wearing', in cat. *The Cauldron*, DeanClough, Henry Moore Institut, Halifax

L. Garner, 'Cops on top in Cauldron', *The Daily Express*, Aug 2, p.40

P. Usherwood, 'The Cauldron', *Art Monthly*, July-Aug, No.198, pp.30-31

J. Hall, 'Letter From London - Towers of London', *Artforum*, Summer, pp.31-33

L. Buck, 'Silver Scene', *Artforum*, Summer, pp.34-36

L. Bang Larsen, 'Traffic', *Flash Art*, No.189, Summer, pp.126-127

G. Walters, 'State of the Art, *The Times Magazine on Saturday*, July 20, pp.27-30

P. Bickers, 'The Young Devils, *Art Press*, No.214, June, pp.34-35

'Imagined Communities', *Blueprint*

'P. Masterson, 'Imagined Communities', *Art Monthly*, No.194, March, pp.33-35

Projects

1994

'Rooseum Video Programme', Rooseum, Center for Contemporary Art, Malmö

'Holly Street Estate Art Project', London

Colophon

Exhibition

Concept
Jan Debbaut
Jaap Guldemond
Selma Klein Essink
Frank Lubbers

Organization
Marente Bloemheuvel
Jaap Guldemond

Catalogue

Editing
Marente Bloemheuvel
Jaap Guldemond

Texts
Adam Chodzko
Lynne Cooke
Jan Debbaut
Jean Fisher
Jaap Guldemond
Mark Kremer
Stéphanie Moisdon
Gregor Muir
Michelle Nicol
Oliver Sacks
Mats Stjernstedt

Biographies — Bibliographies
Diana Franssen

Translations
Nancy Forest-Flier, Alkmaar (Dutch/English)
Donald Gardner (Dutch/English)
Marijke van der Glas, Amsterdam (German/Dutch)
John Rudge (Dutch/English)
Peter Samuelsson (Swedish/English)

Photography
Peter Cox, Eindhoven
Heidi Kosaniuk
Armin Linke, Milan
Andrew Nairne
John Riddy
Edward Woodman

Design
Arlette Brouwers, Amsterdam/Emst

Printing
Lecturis bv, Eindhoven

Acknowledgements

the artists

Alexander and Bonin, New York
Ernst van Alphen, Amsterdam
Bloom Gallery, Amsterdam
Caldic Collection, Rotterdam
Sadie Coles, London
Deitch Projects, New York
Galerie Analix, Geneva
Galerie Anne de Villepoix, Paris
Galerie Fons Welters, Amsterdam
Galerie Ghislaine Hussenot, Paris
Galerie Gisela Capitain, Cologne
Galleri Index, Stockholm
Kerlin Gallery, Dublin
Lisson Gallery, London
Matt's Gallery, London
Maureen Paley/Interim Art, London
Metro Pictures, New York
Thomas Nordanstad Gallery, New York
Anthony Reynolds Gallery, London
Sammlung Goetz, Munich

Texts

Oliver Sacks, *A matter of identity*.
Copyright © Oliver Sacks 1985. Reproduced by
permission of the author c/o Rogers, Coleridge &
White Ltd., 20 Powis Mews, London W11 1JN in
association with International Creative
Management Inc, 40 West 57th Street, New York,
NY 10019 USA. *The man who mistook his wife for a
hat* is published by Picador.

Jean Fisher on Willie Doherty. An extract from an
essay in the exhibition catalogue *Willie Doherty: The
only good one is a dead one*, published by The
Edmonton Art Gallery, Edmonton, Canada, 1996.

Interview Douglas Gordon by Stéphanie Moisdon.
An extract from an interview published in *Blocnotes,
Art contemporain*, No. 11, January-February, 1996.

Mark Kremer on Aernout Mik. This article has been
published in *Artist Kunstmagazin*, No. 27, 2, 1996.

Lynne Cooke on Tony Oursler. This article was
originally published as 'Tony Oursler: Alters' in
Parkett, No.47, September, 1996 (collaboration
Tony Oursler, Raymond Pettibon, Thomas Schütte).

Interview Georgina Starr by Adam Chodzko. An
extract from an interview published in *Tate, The Art
Magazine*, Spring, 1996.

Gregor Muir on Gillian Wearing. A version of this
text was first published as part of the essay 'Winter
1996', *The Cauldron*, The Henri Moore Sculpture
Trust.

Publication rights have been settled as far as
possible. Anyone who feels that his/her rights have
been infringed upon can contact the museum.

ISBN 90-70149-59-1